Social Support
in Couples

**SAGE SERIES ON
CLOSE RELATIONSHIPS**

Series Editors
Clyde Hendrick, Ph.D., and
Susan S. Hendrick, Ph.D.

In this series...

Social Support in Couples

Marriage as a Resource in Times of Stress

Carolyn E. Cutrona

SS
CR
*Sage
Series
on Close
Relationships*

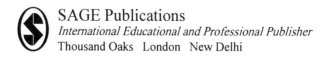

SAGE Publications
International Educational and Professional Publisher
Thousand Oaks   London   New Delhi

For information address:

SAGE Publications, Inc.
2455 Teller Road
Thousand Oaks, California 91320
E-mail: order@sagepub.com

SAGE Publications Ltd.
6 Bonhill Street
London EC2A 4PU
United Kingdom

SAGE Publications India Pvt. Ltd.
M-32 Market
Greater Kailash I
New Delhi 110 048 India

Printed in the United States of America

Library of Congress Cataloging-in-Publication Data

Cutrona, Carolyn E.
    Social support in couples: Marriage as a resource in times of
stress / author, Carolyn E. Cutrona
        p. cm.— (Sage series in close relationships; v. 13)
    Includes bibliographical references and index.
    ISBN 0-8039-4883-2 (cloth: acid-free paper). — ISBN 0-8039-4884-0
(pbk.: acid-free paper).
    1. Interpersonal relations. 2. Marriage—Psychological aspects.
    2. Social networks—Psychological aspects. 4. Stress (Psychology).
    5. Stress management. I. Title. II. Series.
HM132.C87 1996
158'.2—dc20   95-50188

This book is printed on acid-free paper.

96 97 98 99 00 10 9 8 7 6 5 4 3 2 1

Sage Production Editor: Tricia K. Bennett

To Dan, Gina, and Jonathan

Contents

Series Editors' Introduction

When we first began our work on love attitudes more than a decade ago, we did not know what to call our research area. In some ways, it represented an extension of earlier work in interpersonal attraction. Most of our scholarly models were psychologists (although sociologists had long been deeply involved in the areas of courtship and marriage), yet we sometimes felt as if our work had no professional "home." That has all changed. Our research has not only a home but also an extended family, and the family is composed of relationship researchers. During the past decade, the discipline of close relationships (also called personal relationships and intimate relationships) has flourished.

Two aspects of close relationships research should be noted. The first is its rapid growth, resulting in numerous books, journals, handbooks, book series, and professional organizations. As fast as the field grows, the demand for even more research and knowledge seems to be increasing. Questions about close, personal relation-

ships still far exceed answers. The second noteworthy aspect of the
new discipline of close relationships is its interdisciplinary nature.
The field owes its vitality to scholars from communication, family
studies, human development, psychology (clinical, counseling, developmental, social), sociology, and other disciplines such as nursing and social work. This interdisciplinary wellspring gives close
relationships research its diversity and richness, qualities that we
hope to achieve in the current series.

The **Sage Series on Close Relationships** is designed to acquaint
diverse readers with the most up-to-date information about various
topics in close relationships theory and research. Each volume in the
series covers a particular topic in one area of close relationships.
Each book reviews the particular topic area, describes contemporary
research in the area (including the authors' own work, where appropriate), and offers some suggestions for interesting research
questions or real-world applications related to the topic. The volumes
are designed to be appropriate for students and professionals in
communication, family studies, psychology, sociology, and social
work, among others. A basic assumption of the series is that the
broad panorama of close relationships can best be portrayed by
authors from multiple disciplines so that the series cannot be "cap-
tured" by any single disciplinary bias.

Modeling this interdisciplinary emphasis within her career, Carolyn
E. Cutrona, a clinical psychologist, has worked extensively in the
interface of clinical and social psychology with her research on
social support. In the current volume, she applies the extensive
social support literature to married couples and partnered relationships. Nowhere is social support more important than in the long-
term partnered relationships in which we spend much of our lives.

Addressing issues such as the interplay between social support
and conflict during a health crisis, Cutrona skillfully weaves case
examples into her presentation of the most up-to-date research in
the area. The result is an important and much-needed addition to
the social support literature.

CLYDE HENDRICK
SUSAN S. HENDRICK
SERIES EDITORS

❦

Preface

Since 1980, more than 4,000 journal articles have been published on social support. Most of these articles pose the same tired question over and over again: Does social support predict mental or physical health among individuals facing Stressor *X*? Stressor *X* has included childbirth, rape, war, diagnosis of AIDS, heart attack, caregiving for an Alzheimer's patient, unemployment, divorce, and almost any other taxing event one can imagine. Few of these studies have examined what actually goes on between people as they strive to deal together with life's problems. In this book, I have tried to delve into the everyday acts that communicate caring and concern in one specific relationship. I chose marriage because the most important sources of support are the people to whom we are closest. Although the studies I review deal almost exclusively with married couples, I imagine that many, if not all, of the findings apply equally well to other kinds of relationships characterized by commitment and emotional intimacy (e.g., lesbian and gay relationships, close friendships, some parent-child relationships).

The book is appropriate for advanced undergraduate or graduate classes in the areas of close relationships, health psychology, and marital and family studies. It was also written for students and practitioners in the fields of social work, psychology, and marital and family counseling. For researchers, I hope that it provides a useful review of empirical research on the process and consequences of social support in the context of marriage.

Chapter 1 provides an overview of definitions and conceptualizations of social support. A new definition of support that emphasizes responsivity to the other's needs is offered. This definition provides links to other topics in the study of close relationships, including interpersonal attachment. Whereas previous authors have linked social support primarily to the mental and physical health outcomes of individuals, Chapter 1 explores the potential benefits of frequent supportive exchanges to relationships. These include the growth of love, interdependence, trust, and commitment.

In Chapter 2, gender-related differences in social support and coping are considered. Research on the differences between men and women regarding the benefits and costs they derive from the marital relationship is critically examined. More generally, problems that can arise when two people have stylistic differences in dealing with stress are considered—gender related or not.

The step-by-step processes of eliciting, providing, and receiving social support are described in Chapter 3. Factors that influence the decision of whether or not to disclose a stressful event to one's partner are considered as well as factors that influence the decision of whether to provide support once the desire or need for support has been expressed. Factors that influence the perceived helpfulness of support-intended acts are explored.

In Chapter 4, the interplay between supportive and destructive interactions is addressed. A reciprocal relationship is described between supportive and hostile behaviors. For example, supportive acts can prevent the spiraling of marital disagreements into intense destructive fights. On the other hand, disappointed support expectations can lead to resentment and hasten the deterioration of a relationship.

Special problems arise in the mutual give-and-take of social support when one member of a couple has a disabling illness. In Chapter 5, issues that arise when couples face the chronic stress of serious medical illness are discussed. These issues include dealing with anger, maintaining equity, and the dangers of fostering excessive dependence.

Chapter 6 offers suggestions for marital therapists on how to help people increase the quality and frequency of support that they provide to one another. Based on the research summarized in the first five chapters, specific techniques are described for helping partners improve their skills in communicating support to one another, staying emotionally close during crises, and avoiding the pitfalls of excessive dependency.

A research agenda for the future is outlined in Chapter 7. Basic research is needed on how social support fits into the array of close relationship constructs. Longitudinal studies are needed to trace the course of marriages that begin with high versus low levels of support. There is a particular need for observational research to identify the support strategies associated with high versus low levels of marital satisfaction and for tightly controlled support intervention studies.

I have tried to provide a fresh perspective on social support and to suggest new ways that support might influence well-being. Supportive acts have remarkable power, especially when offered by someone we love.

CAROLYN E. CUTRONA

❦

Acknowledgments

I would like to acknowledge with sincere thanks the efforts of Nancy Rosenquist, who provided outstanding secretarial assistance in the preparation of this manuscript. In addition, I would like to thank Kari Dahlin, without whom I would never have finished the reference list.

1

What Is Social Support and What Makes You Think You Have It?

Sue works 40 hours a week in an office job and attends night school, where she is carrying a heavy load of graduate courses. She hopes to complete the course work for her masters in business administration in another 18 months. Sue has been married to Ron for 12 years. They have two daughters, age 8 and 10.

"By the end of the day, I'm totally exhausted," says Sue. "I don't know how I'd survive if it weren't for Ron. A couple of times, I've thought of dropping out of the master's program—it's really high-powered and they try to jam so much information into our heads at one time. I'm competing against kids who are at least 10 years younger than I am! But Ron always tells me I can do it, that I have a lot more business experience than the younger students and I'm underestimating myself. I even believe him, sometimes! He does most of the cooking now, and we decided to hire someone to clean the house once a week, because the little time we have on weekends, we want to spend doing something other than vacuuming and cleaning toilets! He tells the girls that even though I can't spend as much time with them now as I used to, that the whole family should help me so I can finish my degree and get a more interesting job. He says that helping each other to better themselves is part of being in a family. I still feel guilty, but I know I'd feel worse if he complained or accused me of neglecting the kids. He's not a saint or anything, but I just feel like he's totally behind me, and that he'll love me no matter what, and he'll try to help me in every way he can."

1

There are many definitions of social support and many controversies over how social support should be conceptualized and measured. All would agree, however, that the above account describes a supportive relationship.

This chapter briefly describes controversies over the definition of social support; it then provides a working definition of social support that seems to apply to the ongoing give-and-take of support within the context of marital relationships. A major thesis of this book is that intimate relationships are the most important source of social support. The spouse is frequently the first person from whom support is sought during crises (Beach, Martin, Blum, & Roman, 1993; Blood & Wolfe, 1960; Burke & Weir, 1977), and evidence suggests that support from other sources cannot compensate for a lack of intimate or marital support (Brown & Harris, 1978; Coyne & DeLongis, 1986; Lieberman, 1982; O'Hara, 1986). The benefits of a supportive marriage and the costs of an unsupportive marriage are very great indeed. The former can bring years of deeply satisfying interactions and a sense of personal effectiveness and security. The latter can bring extreme loneliness, resentment, and insecurity (Weiss, 1974).

The study of social support has progressed separately from the study of other aspects of close relationships, with a few notable exceptions (Barbee, Druen, Gulley, Yankeelov, & Cunningham, 1993; Coyne & DeLongis, 1986; Duck & Silver, 1990; Gottlieb, 1985; Julien & Markman, 1991). Most research on the benefits of social support has focused on advantages accrued by individuals who receive support from others—better mental health, fewer physical health problems, even lower rates of mortality. The second key theme this book develops is that relationships also benefit from an ongoing exchange of supportive behaviors. Many of the key attributes of successful relationships are fostered by a pattern of mutual supportiveness that is established early and continues throughout the life of the relationship. These attributes include love, interdependence, trust, tolerance, and commitment. Within ongoing relationships such as marriage, the physical and mental health benefits derived from partner support may, in large part, be derived from the positive qualities that supportive acts nourish within the relationship. Interconnections between social support and a range of key relationship characteristics are considered later in this chapter, after a discussion of how best to define social support in the context of ongoing intimate relationships.

ઢ Defining Social Support

All definitions of social support are based on the assumption that people must rely on one another to meet certain basic needs. For some theorists, social support is the fulfillment by others of basic ongoing requirements for well-being. For other theorists, social support is the fulfillment of more specific time-limited needs that arise as the result of adverse life events or circumstances. Each of these perspectives is discussed below.

Fulfillment of Ongoing Interpersonal Needs

The importance of relationships with others for mental health is a key assumption underlying the conceptualization of social support as fulfillment of ongoing social needs (Bowlby, 1969; Weiss, 1974). For example, Weiss (1974) proposes six different functions that are served by relationships with others. He conceptualizes these functions as provisions that are required for well-being. These include attachment (a close relationship that provides security and safety), social integration (a sense of belonging to a group of people with similar interests and concerns), reassurance of worth (recognition of one's skills and competency), guidance (advice and information), reliable alliance (knowledge that another will offer unconditional assistance in times of need), and opportunity to provide nurturing (feeling needed for another's well-being). Caplan (1974) hypothesizes a similar set of basic interpersonal needs, including love and affection, freedom to express personal feelings, validation of personal identity and worth, satisfaction of nurturance and dependency needs, help with tasks, and support in handling emotion and controlling impulses. Social support is defined as access to relationships that meet these kinds of fundamental interpersonal needs (Kaplan, Cassel, & Gore, 1977; Lin, 1986). Kaplan et al.'s (1977) definition of social support exemplifies this tradition: "the

gratification of a person's basic needs (approval, esteem, succor, etc.)
by significant others" (p. 50).

Although terminology differs from theorist to theorist, a core set
of functions served by relationships appears over and over. This core
includes emotional support (expressions of love, empathy, concern),
esteem support (respect for the person's qualities, belief in the
person's abilities, validation of the person's thoughts, feelings, or
actions), information support (factual input, advice, appraisal of the
situation), and tangible assistance (assistance with tasks or physical
resources, such as money or a place to live). Some definitions also
include companionship (shared interests and concerns), although
Rook (1984b) argues against the inclusion of companionship in
conceptualizations of social support. A useful discussion of similarities and differences across categorization systems can be found
in Vaux (1988).

Several features of this approach to defining social support should
be noted. First, the needs addressed by social support are not linked
to crises or adverse life circumstances. Rather, they are conceptualized as ever-present requirements for well-being and adjustment.
Thus, social support is not linked exclusively to crisis situations but
is conceptualized as enhancing the quality of life irrespective of
adversity level. This perspective predicts a "main effect" for social
support—that for persons facing both high and low levels of adversity, those with higher quality social support will enjoy greater
physical and mental health.

Assistance During Times of Adversity

Some researchers have adopted a more focused definition of
social support that emphasizes fulfillment of needs that arise as a
consequence of stressful life events or adverse personal or environmental circumstances. This conceptualization arose in the context of
research on the adverse effects of poor living conditions and stressful life events on mental and physical health (Caplan, 1974; Cassel,
1974; Cobb, 1976). Research revealed that although some people
succumb to illness in the wake of negative life events, many others
do not (Rabkin & Streuning, 1976). A search for factors that might
protect people against the deleterious effects of stress was under-

taken, and high-quality relationships with others were identified as a potential protective factor or buffer. Although no one would deny the value of high-quality relationships when life is proceeding smoothly, the primary emphasis in this approach is on the stress-buffering functions of social support. In other words, the primary benefit to the recipient of social support is protection against the deterioration of health and well-being that would otherwise be caused by the pressures of recent or ongoing stressful events. In this perspective, a moderating effect of social support on outcomes is predicted (i.e., a statistical interaction between stress and social support in the prediction of health outcomes). At low levels of support, those with high levels of stress experience poor mental and physical health outcomes; however, when protected by high levels of support, even those experiencing a high stress load do not succumb to declining health or experience a less severe decline. Another implication of this interaction between stress and social support in the prediction of health is that social support is beneficial only under conditions of high stress—when stress levels are low, social support is unrelated to well-being.

❧ When Does Social Support Exert Its Effect?

A Lifetime of Preparation for Stress

Researchers who emphasize the stress-buffering functions of social support differ in the extent to which they focus on support provided before the onset of life crises (throughout the history of the relationship) versus supportive acts performed after a stressful event has occurred. Both perspectives predict that social support affects health and adjustment primarily in times of adversity. They differ in their time frames. In one perspective, months or years of life with a partner who is sensitively responsive to one's needs gradually strengthens an individual, enabling the individual to cope well when confronted with life crises. In this model, support received from a partner in the context of previous stressful life events bolsters the person's ability to cope with new problems because, for example, the person is confident that he or she is not alone and that others have faith in his or her competence. The work of Cobb exemplifies this approach. According to Cobb (1979), social support should be conceptualized as information leading the person to believe that he or she is "cared for and loved, valued and esteemed, and belongs to a network of mutual obligation" (p. 93). Cobb (1979) believes that relationships that engender these positive beliefs allow people to proceed with steps necessary to solve their problems or to accept unchangeable circumstances with a minimum loss of self-esteem. Such beliefs are not engendered quickly, but require a significant history of interaction.

A variety of mechanisms has been proposed through which a history of supportive interactions may prepare a person to deal with stress. These include the development of self-esteem and self-efficacy beliefs, minimization of interpersonal anxiety, faith in the availability of assistance when it is needed, confirmation and validation of the person's adequacy in valued life roles (e.g., mother, friend), and social control (pressure to avoid risky behavior and engage in health-protective behavior) (Cohen & Wills, 1985; Thoits, 1986).

Parallels should be noted between this discussion of social support and discussions of the self-confidence and security that derive from a high-quality attachment between child and caregiver during development. This theme is further developed in a later section.

Resources for Coping With a Specific Crisis

Social support has been defined by other researchers as transactions that occur after the onset of adverse circumstances. For example, Rook (1984a) describes social support as help-oriented transactions that occur "in response to learning of another's problem" (p. 243). House (1981) urges researchers to think of social support as "who gives what to whom, regarding what problems" (p. 39). He defines social support as a problem-centered interaction involving one or more of the traditional interpersonal support functions (emotional concern, instrumental aid, information). In all these definitions, emphasis is placed on acts that follow the occurrence of a stressful event and that address one or more needs that arose as a consequence of the stressor. Mechanisms through which supportive acts protect against negative outcomes following negative life events include encouragement of health-protective and avoidance of risky behaviors, encouragement of adaptive coping behaviors, situation-specific boosts in self-efficacy, encouragement of realistic appraisals of the situation, modulation of negative affect, and assistance in solving the specific problems that led to distress (e.g., deciding on the best problem-solving approach, working together on tangible aspects of the problem, giving or loaning needed resources). An excellent discussion of such mechanisms can be found in Cohen (1988).

❧ Operationalizing Social Support

Different beliefs about the province of social support lead to different operationalizations of the construct. When qualities of relationships over time are emphasized, it is very difficult to assess social support through any means other than subjective self-reports, although a few attempts have been made to ask persons who know the target person well to evaluate the supportiveness of the target person's relationships with others (Cutrona, 1989). The individual who has experienced a relationship is best qualified to evaluate whether a given relationship meets his or her needs, either longstanding or crisis generated. This approach has been criticized because of its subjectivity and the potential for "contamination" by factors other than experiences with the support provider. For example, the mood or personality of the support recipient may bias his or her assessments of the relationship (Procidano & Heller, 1983). Despite a spouse who objectively provides frequent help-intended behaviors, a low level of supportiveness may be reported by a depressed partner or a partner characterized by a generally negative outlook.

A second question that arises is whether the target person has sufficient information to provide an accurate assessment of another's supportiveness. For example, unless another person has gone through a serious crisis with the target individual, how does the target person know how adequately the potential provider will meet his or her needs in an emergency? Some argue that the belief that others will provide assistance in times of need is beneficial, even if it is an untested or an incorrect assumption (Thoits, 1992; Turner, Frankel, & Levin, 1983). The belief that support resources will be available, if needed, is termed *perceived social support* or *perceived available support* (Dunkel-Schetter & Bennett, 1990). Results across a large number of studies reveal a consistent positive relation between perceived social support and well-being (see meta-analyses by Leppin & Schwarzer, 1990; Schwarzer & Leppin, 1989, 1991).

Researchers who are dissatisfied with the subjectivity, potential inaccuracy, and vulnerability to bias of perceived social support assessments prefer to focus on actual support transactions. In this approach, the target individual is asked to report on more objective indices of support, for example, the frequency of support behaviors received from others in a specified period of time (Barrera & Ainley, 1983). Such measures index a construct that is termed *received social support.* Although still open to self-report distortions, not so much is left to the imagination of the individual because concrete events are the focus of the assessment. Critics of the received support approach argue, however, that the number of recent help-intended behaviors does not provide an index of the quality of support experiences (Turner et al., 1983). Not all attempts at supportiveness are successful. Some are perceived as intrusive, demeaning, or insensitive (Wortman & Lehman, 1985). Thus, the importance of retaining a qualitative or evaluative component in the assessment of social support has been argued (Turner et al., 1983).

Furthermore, number of support behaviors received may be, in part, an index of the severity of the target person's problems or distress. The person's friends and family may simply provide more support when the individual needs it more. This leads to a positive correlation between frequency of support and distress; however, the direction of causality is from distress to support receipt rather than from support receipt to distress. In general, measures of received support correlate less strongly with physical and mental health outcomes than do measures of perceived social support (Wethington & Kessler, 1986). An excellent discussion of the relative advantages and disadvantages of measuring perceived versus received social support can be found in Dunkel-Schetter and Bennett (1990).

More recently, attempts have been made to assess the actual verbal and nonverbal behaviors that occur when one person discloses a stress to another. A few researchers have developed observational coding schemes to gain detailed information about what people say and do in their attempts to be helpful to another person (Barbee, 1990a; Barker, 1984; Cutrona, Suhr, & MacFarlane, 1990; Liotta, Jason, Robinson, & LaVigne, 1985). Such techniques allow researchers to examine the behavioral determinants of the perception that another has been supportive, that is, to examine what kinds of statements and behaviors are associated with high subjective ratings of supportiveness in the context of different kinds of stressful events (Cutrona & Suhr, 1992). It is hoped that observational techniques will also be useful as a basis for the design of social support interventions, in that specific types of support communications can be tested regarding their utility in easing symptoms of depression, anxiety, loneliness, and other manifestations of distress.

ೱ Related Constructs: Social Integration and Social Networks

The term *social support* is sometimes applied to constructs that should properly be termed *social integration* or *social networks.* Social integration (also termed *social involvement*) reflects the presence or absence of key social ties, most often marriage and membership in groups such as churches, clubs, and other voluntary organizations. Social integration is an important construct because the absence of such ties (social isolation) is a serious health risk factor. A series of large-scale epidemiological studies has documented a two- to fivefold greater risk for mortality among socially isolated persons over a 3- to 10-year time span (e.g., Berkman & Breslow, 1983).

The social network approach involves more detailed quantitative assessments of the individual's social ties. A person's social network includes the people with whom he or she interacts on a regular basis (e.g., friends, neighbors, coworkers, family members). Many different parameters of the social network are assessed, including number of network members, strength of ties to network members (e.g., close or strong ties versus casual or weak ties), the composition of the network (e.g., kin versus nonkin), density of the network (how many network members know each other), proximity to network members, and frequency of contact with network members. Social network indices are related in an important way to social support. Members of the social network are potential sources of social support. Although a large social network does not ensure that the key functions of social relationships (e.g., attachment, guidance, reassurance of worth, tangible assistance) will be provided to the target person, there is generally a significant positive relation between, for example, network size and perceived social support (Cutrona, 1986). In other words, the probability of receiving support increases as a function of number of social ties.

◈ Social Support in the Context of Marriage

In the example provided at the beginning of the chapter, Sue faces the crisis of returning to graduate school while working full-time and filling the roles of both wife and mother. She describes many things that her husband, Ron, has done to make this stressful period easier to bear. In addition, she describes qualities of the relationship that have sustained her for many years, not just in times of crisis. The working definition of social support I use in this discussion recognizes both the cumulative benefits over time of supportive interactions (e.g., a sense of security and self-efficacy) and fulfillment of immediate needs engendered by stressful life events (e.g., help in deciding how to deal with a difficult instructor). For the purposes of the current discussion, social support is conceptualized most generally as responsiveness to another's needs and, more specifically, as acts that communicate caring; that validate the other's worth, feelings, or actions; or that facilitate adaptive coping with problems through the provision of information, assistance, or tangible resources.

The key concept of *responsiveness* is particularly important. Theoretical and empirical literature highlight the psychological significance of responsivity to one's needs by the social environment. For example, responsive caregiving is viewed by attachment theorists as the cornerstone of the bond that grows between infant and caregiver in the earliest months of life and shapes the child's beliefs about the essential goodness of both the self and others (Ainsworth, Blehar, Waters, & Wall, 1978; Bowlby, 1969). In adult relationships, expectations that form the core of trust are those that focus on the partner's responsiveness to one's needs in situations of stress (Holmes & Rempel, 1989). Attitudes of trust reflect the expectation that the partner can be relied on to care for one and to be responsive to one's needs, now and in the future. The importance of perceiving the environment as contingently responsive to one's actions plays a prominent role in current theories of depression (Abramson, Metalsky, & Alloy, 1989; Abramson, Seligman, & Teasdale, 1978). According to such theories, the belief that one is not able to influence the occurrence of negative or positive events in one's life leads to feelings of depression, whereas the belief that one can influence events protects against the onset of depression following adverse events. An important source of information about the extent to which a person can influence his or her world is the behavior of significant others, including their responsiveness to the individual's needs in times of stress.

Conceptualizing social support as acts that reflect responsivity to another's needs opens the door to connections with many other constructs within the field of close relationships. Some of these connections are described in the following section. Although many of these connections are speculative at this time, it is hoped that in highlighting theoretically based links, researchers will be stimulated to conduct relevant empirical tests. It is also hoped that by drawing such connections, a richer context for thinking about the potential implications of social support for close relationships will be provided.

⅍ A Place for Social Support in the Study of Close Relationships

Social Support in the Development of Relational Schemas

Acts that communicate concern ("Are you sure you're OK? Why don't you lie down for a few minutes?"), reassurance ("Don't be so hard on yourself—you're a wonderful mother!"), understanding ("I understand why you're disappointed; you were counting the days until your sister's visit."), and willingness to help ("I wish you'd let me carry the heavier boxes; your back hurt you for weeks after we

moved the last time.") can have consequences far beyond the immediate situations in which they occur. Such supportive acts not
only ease the distress and burden of the immediate moment, but
they also contribute to the recipient's view of his or her relationship
with the provider. In other words, a series of interactions in which
another consistently behaves supportively leads to the formation of
a picture or schema of the relationship as one in which support is
forthcoming when needed. (See Baldwin, 1992, and Planalp, 1987,
for a discussion of relational schemas. See also Beach, Fincham,
Katz, & Bradbury, in press.)

Berscheid (1994) highlights the importance of relational schemas
that concern whether or not an individual can be counted on for
support. According to Berscheid, a crucial dimension of how people
evaluate their relationship with their intimate partner is whether or
not that person will provide support when needed:

> [An] array of theories and evidence on security and trust strongly
> suggest that expectations concerning whether care will be received
> from the relationship partner in response to need may be an impor-
> tant component of most relationship schemas. It may even be the
> central component—one that is present in every developed relation-
> ship schema and one that will exert special influence on all other
> components of the schema. (p. 104)

Feeling emotionally supported ranks as one of the primary expectations for intimate relationships (Baxter, 1986; Braiker & Kelley,
1979; Newcomb, 1990). The disappointment of support expectations
can be highly destructive to intimate relationships. Former relationship partners cited lack of support as a critical cause of the dissolution of their relationships in a study of expectations in relationship
maintenance (Baxter, 1986). Baxter (1986) concludes that the expectation of support from an intimate partner has the status of a
"relationship rule": Partners believe they should be supportive of
each other, and when this rule is broken, the relationship itself is
threatened.

The survival of intimate relationships, including the marital relationship, thus may be partially dependent on the exchange of supportive acts, which contributes to a relational schema that includes
belief in the partner's responsivity in times of need. In the following

section, theoretical links between supportive acts, relational schemas, and qualities of relationships that are critical for their survival are described.

Social Support and
the Development of Close Relationships

Many important attributes of close relationships appear to have close ties to social support. In fact, their development is hard to imagine in the absence of a consistent exchange of supportive acts. These attributes include love, interdependence, trust, and commitment.

Love

People fall in love for many reasons—physical attraction, shared interests, reflection of a valued self-image, the pleasures of quiet companionship. For love to survive, however, theorists emphasize the importance of concern for the other's needs and striving to meet those needs (Kelley, 1983; Maslow, 1968; Rubin, 1973a, 1973b). Caring—defined as wanting to help the other by providing aid and emotional support whenever needed—is included in most conceptualizations of love (Hendrick & Hendrick, 1992). The importance of caring in people's conceptualizations or prototypes of love was demonstrated by Steck, Levitan, McLane, and Kelley (1982). These researchers created different profiles of individuals' feelings for their romantic partner. These profiles differed with respect to the proportion of items endorsed that described need for the partner (e.g., "If I could never be with ____, I would feel miserable.") and those that de-scribed caring for the partner (e.g., "If ____ were feeling badly, my first duty would be to cheer him/her up."). Research participants rated the degree to which the individuals who completed the profiles loved their partners. Results revealed that those with a high proportion of care items were judged to love their partners the most. Need items correlated most strongly with judgments of attraction, but care items correlated most strongly with judgments of love. Based on these results and others, Kelley (1983) concludes that care is the central component of current views of love. The care component—which overlaps virtually completely with the definition of social support as responsivity to the other's needs—forms the core of people's commonsense understanding of love. If over time an individual does not see evidence of such responsivity in an intimate partner, that individual will have difficulty maintaining the belief that the partner really loves him or her. Such doubts may seriously undermine the strength of the relationship and may quickly erode its foundation. In contrast, an individual who sees ample evidence of responsivity to his or her needs by the partner is likely to form a relational schema that includes both supportiveness and love.

Interdependence

The relationship between two people is described as highly interdependent when, over a prolonged period of time, the activities of each person have strong and frequent impact on those of the other person across many domains of the individuals' lives. In other words, the thoughts, feelings, and behaviors of each person are strongly influenced by the other. Interdependence is an important predictor of relationship survival. In a study by Berscheid, Snyder, and Omoto (1989), only interdependence predicted the persistence over time of relationships between dating couples. Variables that did not attain significance included duration of the relationship, ratings of relationship satisfaction, and subjective closeness ratings. Within a developing intimate relationship, supportive behaviors may contribute to the growth of interdependence. When an individual is responsive to the needs of his or her partner, the partner's outcomes will be positively affected—that is, he or she will feel better, cope better, and perform better. This kind of positive interdependence may contribute to relationship survival directly or through the mediation of trust and commitment, both of which are discussed below.

Trust

In close relationships, trust has been conceptualized as the confident expectation that positive outcomes will be forthcoming from one's partner (Holmes & Rempel, 1989). According to Holmes and

Rempel (1989), "expectations that form the core of trust are those that focus on the partner's responsiveness to one's needs in situations of dependency" (p. 188). As relationships progress, individuals become increasingly interdependent in a greater number of domains and at deeper levels (Levinger, 1983). As people realize the extent to which their lives are intertwined and the degree to which they are dependent on the other's goodwill, they often experience concern and feelings of vulnerability (Eidelson, 1980). Kelley and Thibaut (1978) describe the development of trust as a gradual process of uncertainty reduction—in the case of close relationships, the reduction of uncertainty about the strength of the relationship. Will the partner continue to behave in ways that reflect genuine caring and concern? Is it "safe" to let down one's guard and reveal vulnerable aspects of oneself? Holmes and Rempel emphasize the importance of supportive acts in the development of trust—acts that communicate intrinsic motivation to be responsive and caring. If the partner is consistently responsive to the individual's needs, even when such responsivity requires personal inconvenience or sacrifice, the individual may eventually develop a schema of the relationship as trustworthy.

Once such trust is established, the relationship is on much more secure footing than prior to the establishment of trust. The relationship is transformed from an "exchange" relationship, in which prompt repayment is expected for favors or services, to a "communal" relationship, in which each person expects that needs will be met as they arise with no expectation of immediate repayment (Clark & Mills, 1979). A second critically important consequence of trust is that negative acts by the partner are much diminished in terms of the damage they inflict on the relationship (Holmes & Rempel, 1989). Because the partner is viewed as committed to one's welfare and to the relationship, even behavior that contradicts this view does not change one's core beliefs about the partner. For example, if the partner forgets to call when he or she is going to be late for dinner or neglects to perform introductions at a party—these acts are not viewed as evidence that he or she "doesn't care." Instead, they are viewed as temporary deviations from an overall pattern of consideration. Attributions are likely to be made to transitory situational causes: "She was uncomfortable with those people and felt so self-conscious that she forgot to introduce me." When a person feels a high level of trust in his or her partner, the person no longer needs proof of the partner's love or commitment. In contrast, when a person feels only a moderate level of trust, all behavior is subject to scrutiny. A high level of vigilance is maintained to determine whether or not the partner can be trusted. As a result, negative behaviors are viewed as highly diagnostic of the partner's true feelings and lead to an erosion of the partner's image (Holmes & Rempel, 1989). Small transgressions take on great symbolic importance: "You didn't introduce me to your boss because you're ashamed of me. You think you're better than me and that I'll drag you down if people know you're married to me!"

Thus, it appears that a consistent pattern of supportive behaviors contributes to the establishment of trust, which has important implications for the emotional tone of the relationship. Consistent support leads to relatively calm sailing, whereas inconsistency or a lack of supportiveness can lead to perpetually stormy seas that may eventually wreck the relationship.

Commitment

Consistent responsivity to the partner's needs fosters not only trust but also commitment. Commitment refers to a person's intention to remain in a relationship no matter what happens—for better or for worse. Kelley (1983) hypothesizes that the critical determinant of commitment is the consistent subjective appraisal, over time, that the rewards of remaining in the relationship outweigh the costs. Certainly one relevant reward is partner supportiveness in times of need. One of the costs of leaving relationships is also relevant to social support—losing the "investment" that one has made over the years in providing support to one's partner. After expending considerable effort trying to meet the needs of one's partner, to leave the relationship means that one's efforts were meaningless—that no long-term rewards or gratifications will result from those efforts. Thus, both receiving support and providing support appear to play a role in the development of commitment.

❧ Conclusions

Social support has been defined as acts that demonstrate responsivity to another's needs. In the context of ongoing relationships such as marriage, support can both prepare a person to deal with future stressors and help a person deal with crises after they occur. It seems likely that demonstrations of responsivity to an individual's needs on a daily basis, when dealing with minor hassles, can translate into a relational schema that includes caring, interdependence, trust, and commitment. When the person later meets a severe crisis, it is in the context of such a highly developed relationship. Social support may influence mental and physical health, in part indirectly, through its enhancement of relationship quality.

2

Gender-Related Differences in Social Support and Coping

Sally confided in her friend, Eve, "I don't know what I'm doing wrong. Bill didn't tell me for a whole week that he didn't get the promotion he'd been hoping for. He claims he wanted to handle it on his own. Why did we get married if he wants to handle things on his own?"

"Honey, you're just getting yourself more upset by talking about it," said Bob to his wife, Virginia. "If your poem is accepted for publication—great! If it's not, then maybe it wasn't that good. You can always write another one. But you're telling everybody who will listen how worried you are that it won't be accepted. I really think you're making it harder on yourself."

Imagine two people who have been raised in different cultures. In one culture, caring, nurturing, and responsibility for others are highly valued. Interdependence rather than independence is stressed. Putting aside personal desires for the well-being of the larger community is taught as an ideal toward which to strive. In the other culture, personal achievement is valued above all. Competition is viewed as healthy, in that it stimulates effort and personal excellence. Self-reliance is very important, and it is considered a sign of weakness to rely on others.

Now imagine what would happen if a person raised in the first culture and a person raised in the second culture were bound together for life and were expected to rely on each other to meet their needs. Several predictions are obvious:

- They will have problems understanding each other's behavior.
- They will suffer confusion or resentment over demands made on them by the other.
- They will experience feelings of rejection or lack of appreciation.

Although an obvious exaggeration, the above "clashing cultures" example makes vivid some of the issues that arise when a woman and a man try to live together after many years of exposure to cultural forces that encourage males and females to develop different viewpoints, values, and skills (see also Derlega, Metts, Petronio, & Margulis, 1993).

Several key differences have been found between husbands and wives in the extent to which they rely on each other for support, the quantity and quality of support they provide, and the strategies they use to cope with stressful life events. The first section of this chapter summarizes research findings on gender differences in the extent to which men versus women benefit from being married—the extent to which marriage predicts better physical and mental health for each gender. The second section considers the relative sensitivity of husbands versus wives to variations in marital quality—the extent to which marital satisfaction, intimacy, and supportiveness are linked to psychological adjustment. The third section addresses differences in the amount and quality of social support that is provided by husbands versus wives in the context of marriage. After a discussion of various explanations for observed gender differences in these domains, the focus shifts from social support to coping. Differences between men and women in typical ways of appraising and dealing with stressful life events are considered. The implications of such differences for coping with adversity as a couple are discussed.

❧ Who Benefits From Marriage?

A large number of studies have shown that, on the average, people who are married are happier, are more satisfied with their lives, enjoy better physical and mental health, are less likely to commit suicide, are less likely to be institutionalized for mental illness or problem behavior, and are less likely to die within a 10-year period than people who are not married (Gove, Hughes, & Style, 1983). These differences are found among people of all ages, races, and income levels. Gove et al. (1983) conducted analyses to determine whether these differences could be explained as an artifact of who succeeds in attracting and retaining a marital partner, that is, those who are physically and psychologically healthiest, most attractive, most socially skilled. In their analyses, controlling for these kinds of variables did not eliminate the beneficial effects of marriage. Marriage truly seems to enhance quality of life.

There is growing evidence, however, that men and women are affected differently by marriage. Marriage is a stronger predictor among men than among women of happiness, satisfaction with home life, and measures of mental health (Gove et al., 1983). In a large longitudinal study of health and mortality, Berkman and Syme (1979) found that marital status was much more strongly predictive of physical health for men than for women. During the 9-year study period, men who were married were much less likely to die than those who were not married; the effects of marriage on mortality among women were much weaker. Married men are happier than married women; however, there is little difference in the happiness levels of never-married men versus never-married women (Gove et al., 1983; Vanfossen, 1986). Antonucci and Akiyama (1987) found that, on the average, men are more satisfied with their marriages than women and they are more reliant on marriage for happiness than women. Women are less satisfied with their marriages, but marital status does not appear to be as critical to their adjustment (Antonucci & Akiyama, 1987).

Does this mean that the marital relationship is not important for women? No! For women, however, simply being married is not enough. The quality of the marital relationship is extremely important. For women, the relation between marital satisfaction and virtually all aspects of mental health is very strong—significantly stronger than for men (Gove et al., 1983). In a sample of married men and women residing in a rural area, marital satisfaction, spouse satisfaction, and spouse availability as a confidant were more powerfully associated with mental health status among women than among men (Husaini, Neff, Newbrough, & Moore, 1982). Similar results were found in a large urban sample (Gove et al., 1983). Thus, it appears that marital status is more important for men than for women, but that marital quality is more important for women than for men. After an overview of research on the social support resources available to men versus women in the context of marriage, I will offer several hypotheses to explain the apparent contradiction that men benefit more than women from being married and suffer more from lack of a marital partner, but that women benefit more from a high-quality marital relationship and suffer more from a poor-quality marriage.

❧ Gender Differences in Sources of Social Support

Men rely more heavily on their spouses for social support than do women. Whereas men depend primarily on their spouses for support, women depend on a variety of sources, including friends, relatives, and neighbors (Antonucci & Akiyama, 1987; Kohen, 1983; Veroff, Kulka, & Douvan, 1981). In a community sample of married men age 50 and older, 82% of the men reported that they confide in their wives; only 63% of women said they confide in their husbands (Antonucci & Akiyama, 1987). Of the men, 74% said they talk to their wives when upset, but only 48% of the women said they talk to their husbands when they are upset. Among adult students returning to college, 83% of the men but only 56% of the women listed their spouses as their greatest sources of emotional support (Huston-Hoburg & Strange, 1986). A lopsided situation exists in which men rely much more heavily and exclusively on their spouses for support than do women.

Prohibitions Against
Support Seeking Among Men

Men are socialized to present the appearance of mastery and control (O'Neil, 1981); thus, when they encounter problems, they may strive to conceal from others the fact that they are having difficulty. I have found that the most frequent strategy for soliciting social support from another person is simply to describe the problem that is causing distress (Cutrona, Suhr, et al., 1990). If a person is unwilling to admit that a situation is problematic, then even those who would be willing to provide support will not be aware of the need. A second strategy for eliciting support from others is to describe one's emotional state—the distress that one is experiencing (Cutrona, Suhr, et al., 1990). The expression of emotions among men in American culture has been characterized as highly restricted (DePaulo, 1982; O'Neil, 1981). Men may find it difficult, embarrassing, or inappropriate to express emotions such as fear, self-doubt, anxiety, and sadness that would act as signals to members of their social network that they are in need of support. There is evidence that the expression of emotional distress by men may be punished by network members. In a study of upper-level businessmen, Weiss (1985) found that the environment seemed to prohibit or punish the display of emotions other than anger in the workplace. If a man tries to seek support, he may be rejected, shunned, or reprimanded by his colleagues for expressing vulnerability.

It has been hypothesized that men solve the dilemma of cultural prohibitions against public behaviors that signal a need for social support by limiting such behaviors to private settings, especially the home. This may be one reason why men are more dependent on marriage for well-being than women are. Whereas women can seek social support from friends and family, men may not have, or may not believe that they have, the option of seeking support from sources other than an intimate female partner.

Women Have Multiple Sources of Social Support

Women are much more likely to have close confiding relationships with persons outside the marital relationship than men are (Lowenthal & Haven, 1968). Women differ from men particularly in the nature of their relationships with friends and the availability of support from friends. Among college students, although men and women did not differ in total number of friends, women were more likely than men to receive emotional support from their friends (Hirsch, 1979; Stokes & Wilson, 1984; Vaux, 1985). Among adult returning students, women reported receiving more support from friends and classmates than did men (Huston-Hoburg & Strange, 1986). Similarly, mothers received more support from friends than fathers in a study of parents of children with cancer (Chesler & Barbarin, 1984).

For a woman with a rich and varied support network, the absence of a marital partner does not leave her without support resources. If a woman has a variety of support sources, she may even choose specific sources for specialized kinds of support. For example, she may turn to a close friend who is an especially good listener when she needs to vent her hurt or frustration; she may turn to her mother for advice on how to deal with a child's behavior problems; she may turn to a friend at work for validation of her dissatisfaction with some aspect of her job.

Although women do have alternative sources of social support, women appear to pay a heavy price for their support resources. Women not only enjoy the benefits of multiple support providers; they also bear the burden of multiple support responsibilities (Belle, 1982). These responsibilities weigh heavily on women. One reason that women have higher rates of depression than men appears to be that their mood is affected not only by stresses in their own lives but also by stresses in the lives of those in their social networks (family, friends, work associates) (Kessler & McLeod, 1984). Men do not appear to be as vulnerable to depression following negative events in the lives of other people.

Despite the fact that women can turn to their mothers, sisters, and close friends for support, the availability of social support from sources outside the marriage does not appear to compensate psychologically for the strain of a poor quality marriage. Among women, psychological adjustment and well-being are closely linked to the level of support received within the marital relationship. In fact, seeking support from sources outside the marriage in the context of a troubled marital relationship was associated with poorer mental health outcomes in a study by Julien and Markman (1991). The relative importance of marital social support for the well-being of men versus women is considered further in a subsequent section.

❧ Gender Differences in the Provision of Marital Social Support

It appears that, on average, men receive more social support from the marital relationship than women do. Belle (1982) describes a *support gap* in male-female relationships: The woman receives less support from her male partner than she provides to him. More husbands than wives report being understood and affirmed by their spouses (Campbell, Converse, & Rodgers, 1976; Vanfossen, 1981). Among married men and women age 50 and older, women received less than men of each of the following from their spouses: confiding, reassuring, respect, sick care, talk when upset, and talk about health (Antonucci & Akiyama, 1987). Wives are more likely to express appreciation to their husbands and offer help with family problems (Vanfossen, 1986). Among couples in which the wife was diagnosed with breast cancer, a number of comparisons were made between the overall support provided by and received from each spouse. Components of support included perceived emotional, appraisal, information, and instrumental support. Both spouses agreed that wives gave more support than they received from their husbands and that husbands received more than they gave in all categories (Vinokur & Vinokur-Kaplan, 1990).

Support for the notion that women provide higher quality social support than men comes from a study of loneliness conducted by Wheeler, Reis, and Nezlek (1983). In this study, male and female college seniors were asked to record and rate every social interaction in which they engaged for a 2-week period. The gender of each interaction partner was recorded, along with several indices of the quality of the interaction. The authors found that amount of time spent interacting with females was a strong negative predictor of loneliness for both males and females; the more time students spent with women, the less lonely they were. The overall quality or meaningfulness of interactions was significantly higher when at least one woman participated in it. All indices of quality were lowest when the interaction was between two males. The same qualities of interactions were important to the well-being of both males and females, but these qualities were more likely to be present when one of the interaction participants was female.

✿ Are the Effects of Social Support on Well-Being Different for Men and Women?

A relatively small number of studies has compared men and women on the effects of spousal social support. In a sample of rural men and women, marital quality and perceived spouse availability as a confidant buffered the effects of negative life events for women only (Husaini et al., 1982). Among women who experienced a high level of stressful life events, social support from the spouse predicted lower levels of depression. The data suggest that among rural men, however, personal competence is more important in dealing with stress than spousal support. In fact, among those men who rated themselves low on personal competence, social support was associated with higher levels of depression. Men who saw themselves as failures may have been humiliated by their reliance on others or by others' efforts to assist them. Among parents of medically ill children, social support effects do not differ for men and women during the acute phase of their child's illness. When the child is in remission or recovered, however, intimacy with a spouse has a stronger protective effect against depression for women than it does for men (Hobfoll, 1991). In a large community sample, the effects of perceived family support were somewhat different for married men and women (Billings & Moos, 1982). In Billings and Moos's (1982) study, family support was defined as perceived cohesion, freedom to express emotions, and lack of conflict in the household. For both men and women, family support was negatively correlated with depression in cross-sectional analyses. In longitudinal analyses, however, changes in perceived family social support predicted changes in depression only among women (both those who worked outside the home and those who did not). Changes in perceived family support did not predict changes in depression among men.

Although there is some evidence that marital social support is more closely linked to well-being for women than for men, such differences are not found in all studies. For example, in a large community sample of midwestern residents, some of whom suffered significant damage in the 1993 floods, marital warmth and supportiveness assessed before the flood predicted lower levels of depression after the flood among both men and women (Freedman, 1995).

*Do Men and Women Benefit
From Different Types of Support?*

It is possible that different components of support are more beneficial to one gender than the other. It was difficult to locate studies in which multiple components of spousal social support were tested as predictors of well-being for men versus women. Two such studies were located, however; they are described below.

Multiple components of marital social support were assessed as predictors of depressive symptoms in a large urban sample of married men and women (Vanfossen, 1981, 1986). Affirmation—the belief that one's spouse appreciates one as one is and helps one to be the kind of person one wants to be—was clearly the most important facet of spousal social support for women. Both women who were employed outside the home and those who were not evidenced less depression if they perceived a high level of affirmation support from their husbands. The status of women is lower than that of men in traditional culture. Thus, respect and affirmation from the husband may be especially important. For nonemployed women, who often lack external feedback on the worth of their activities, the husband may be a critically important source of affirmation that their contributions as wife, mother, and, frequently, nonpaid community volunteer are worthwhile.

Among women who were employed outside the home, tangible assistance from the spouse with household chores and problems emerged as a significant predictor of depression. Women who worked outside the home were less likely to be depressed if they perceived their husbands as contributing significantly to the care of home and children. Research shows that working women still carry the majority of household responsibilities, so assistance that reduces their responsibilities may be especially welcome.

Among men, both affirmation and perceived intimacy with the spouse significantly predicted lower levels of depression. Intimacy was operationalized as being able to talk to the spouse, receiving affection from the spouse, and evaluating the spouse as a good sexual partner. Surprisingly, intimacy did not predict lower levels of depression for women. As discussed previously, opportunities for emotional intimacy for men are very limited outside their relationships with women (Weiss, 1985). Because men are expected to behave independently and to maintain an image of being in control, few acceptable outlets exist for expressions of vulnerability. Thus, the marital relationship may take on extra importance as a source of emotional support.

The inclusion of a satisfying sexual relationship as part of social support is an unusual feature of the Vanfossen (1981, 1986) study. Marital closeness and enjoyment of the sexual relationship appear to have a reciprocal relationship. Sexuality is interpreted as an expression of emotional closeness, especially in middle-class samples (Rainwater, 1969). In a study of 631 couples, correlations of about .50 were found for both men and women between satisfaction with the sexual relationship and perceived emotional supportiveness of the spouse (Schenk, Pfrang, & Rausche, 1983). Emotional supportiveness correlated more highly with sexual satisfaction than did any other variable assessed, including spouse behavior in conflicts, openness, and refusal to provide support.

Schenk et al. (1983) found that the sexual relationship was rated as more important by men than women and that qualitative ratings of the sexual relationship were more strongly correlated with marital happiness for men than for women. Thus, it is possible that in the Vanfossen study (1981, 1986), inclusion of satisfaction with the sexual relationship in the marital intimacy index accounts in part for the stronger correlation between intimacy and depression for men.

The second study comes from my own laboratory (Cutrona & Suhr, 1992, 1994). In an intensive study of social support in the context of marriage, we recruited 50 couples from married student housing at two different midwestern universities. Couples completed a multidimensional questionnaire measure of perceived spousal social support. In addition, each couple participated in an observational assessment of the supportiveness of their interactions. Participants took turns disclosing current sources of distress or concern to their partners. These interactions were videotaped and the behavior of the spouse who was in the role of listener was coded using the Social Support Behavior Code (SSBC) (Cutrona & Suhr, 1992; Suhr, 1990). The SSBC was designed to provide a measure of the frequency and type of social support observed during dyadic interactions. After each disclosure segment, the discloser was asked to complete a measure of satisfaction with the interaction. Couples were recontacted 6 months later and administered a follow-up depression inventory.

We first tested the extent to which specific components of perceived social support predicted level of depressive symptoms 6 months later. For the sample as a whole, when controlling for initial depression and all the other support components, both attachment (emotional support) and guidance (information support) from the spouse predicted lower levels of depression at the follow-up assessment. The central question was whether any of the six social provisions would show a stronger link to Time 2 depression for men or for women. None of the support components interacted significantly with gender. For both men and women, emotional support and information support from the partner were associated with lower levels of subsequent depression.

We conducted analyses to determine whether gender differences would emerge in the specific types of support behaviors (as rated by observers on the SSBC) that predicted interaction satisfaction in the self-disclosure task. For the sample as a whole, only number of emotional and tangible support behaviors contributed significantly to interaction satisfaction. Tests for interactions between gender of recipient and number of support behaviors received were all nonsignificant. Thus, the same kinds of objectively identified support behaviors predicted interaction satisfaction for husbands and wives.

Men and women differed somewhat in the kinds of social support that appeared most important to their well-being in the Vanfossen (1981, 1986) study (i.e., tangible support was more important for employed women than for men and intimacy was more important for men than for women), although affirmation (esteem support) was important for both genders. In my research, no gender differences were found in the components of spousal support that were predictive of adjustment or interaction satisfaction. Cohort or demographic differences between the two samples may account for the differences between the patterns of results found in the two studies. In addition, components of support were operationalized somewhat differently (e.g., intimacy and attachment). It would be premature to draw firm conclusions at this time about differences between the social support needs of men and women because so little research has been conducted on specific components of marital support. Given the differences in the way that men and women are socialized in our society, however, certain kinds of support may be more easily accepted and used by each gender. Further research is needed on the manner in which men and women perceive and react to different kinds of supportive acts.

❧ Returning to the Puzzle: Marital Status Versus Marital Quality

A complex pattern of findings has been described regarding the relative benefits of marriage for men and women, the relative sensitivity of men and women to variations in marital quality, and the social support resources available to and needed by married men versus women. To summarize briefly, men appear to benefit more from marriage than do women, both in physical health and psychological well-being. Once married, it appears that women are more sensitive to the quality of the marital relationship than men are. Stronger associations are found between marital satisfaction and psychological adjustment among women than among men. Men appear to rely very heavily, sometimes exclusively, on their wives for social support. In contrast, a smaller proportion of women consider their husbands their primary sources of support. Women receive support from a much wider range of sources, especially from family and friends. Nevertheless, there is evidence that women are no less sensitive (and perhaps more sensitive) to social support deficits in the marital relationship.

How can the apparent contradictions described above be explained? In particular, why do women benefit less from marriage yet react more strongly to poor quality in the marital relationship? Several possible explanations are considered.

First, it appears that, on average, women are better sources of social support than men. Virtually every study that examined the perceived or received support given by and received from men and women suggests that women are excellent sources of all kinds of social support. They are judged by observers to be more skillful in supportive transactions (Sarason, Sarason, Hacker, & Basham, 1985); the support they provide is more likely to alleviate loneliness and promote well-being (Wheeler et al., 1983); and in the context of both friendship and marriage, they give more support to others than do men.

If one accepts Weiss's (1985) premise that supportive relationships with others are critical for well-being, then it is easy to explain why marriage is more beneficial to men than to women: Men marry women! For men, marriage brings with it a partner who has been trained and shaped throughout her life to provide help and nurturance to others. She has had practice in providing support to close friends and family members for many years and is told in traditional circles that providing encouragement, ego bolstering, and unconditional love is her proper role in the marital relationship. Men who are not married or not involved in an ongoing relationship with a female are inhibited for several reasons from obtaining this kind of support from other sources. They are socialized to conceal difficulties and neediness from others. Furthermore, they may lack the interpersonal skills to elicit support from others, even if they would like to seek support. Thus, men may suffer more from the absence of an intimate partner because, on the average, women are excellent sources of emotional, esteem, and tangible support that is not available elsewhere.

Women, of course, marry men. On the average, men are not as skillful at the provision of social support as women. They have spent years experiencing companionship that centers around shared activities but involves little self-disclosure, emotional expression, or emotional support. They have been socialized that it is a sign of weakness to ask for assistance or to show a need for support. Thus, marriage may not provide the rich social support resources to women that it provides to men. Because women derive support from friends and family members, they may not experience marriage as providing a large increment in support resources. In the absence of a marital partner, they may still have access to relationships with friends and relatives that provide them with sensitive and caring support.

But the puzzle remains: If women have support sources outside the marital relationship, why are they more—not less—affected emotionally by the quality of the marital relationship? Several explanations are possible.

Social Comparison

As a result of long years of experience with mutual exchanges of confidences and support with female friends and relatives, a woman may expect the same quality of exchange with her male partner. Her level of comparison may be established in the context of her prior close relationships with other females. Thus, her history of intimacy with friends may raise her expectations for the quality of the relationship she anticipates with her husband. High-quality relationships with close friends may not serve to lessen her dependence on her husband for support, but may heighten the standard to which she holds the marital relationship. The marital relationship is accorded special status in our culture and the woman may feel intense disappointment unless it equals or surpasses other relationships in her life in quality and supportiveness. It could be argued that men are less likely to have had the same history of highly supportive friendships and are thus unlikely to experience disappointment when comparing the marital relationship to other relationships they have experienced. Such a social comparison process may account, in part, for men's greater satisfaction with their marriages when compared to women. In addition, it may account in part for the somewhat weaker links between quality of the marital relationship and well-being among men.

Different Needs or Different Distributions?

Differences in the variability of support resources supplied by husbands versus wives may contribute to differences between men and women in the association between spousal support and well-being. Belle (1987) suggests that a "ceiling effect" may operate; the average wife may provide such a high level of social support to her husband that further increments in supportiveness may be of little consequence. From a statistical perspective, this restriction of range would result in low or nonsignificant correlations between wife supportiveness and husband well-being. Men may vary more in the level of support they provide to their wives. The average level of support provided by men is lower, which may reflect groups of men at both the very low end and the very high end of the supportiveness continuum. This broader range of male-provided support could result in higher correlations for women between spouse supportiveness and well-being. This explanation of the higher correlation between marital support and well-being for women differs from theories that posit different support needs for men and women. Similar needs may exist for both genders; correlations with outcome variables may differ as a function of differences in the variability of support provided by women versus men in marriage.

Marriage May Hold
More Negatives for Women

It is possible that negative partner behaviors, not variations in positive behaviors, account for the stronger links among women between marital satisfaction and psychological health. Women may be more vulnerable to conflict in the marital relationship. For example, among midwestern flood victims, both men and women were protected against depressive symptoms by marital warmth and supportiveness. Among women only, however, marital hostility was associated with worse outcomes. Women who suffered flood damage and who perceived their husbands as hostile experienced higher levels of postflood depression than those who did not perceive their husbands as hostile (Freedman, 1995). This pattern of results was not found among men. One reason for the greater vulnerability of women to negative marital relationships may be their greater susceptibility to physical abuse. There is a need for studies that assess systematically the relative impact of marital supportiveness and marital conflict in the prediction of psychological adjustment among men and women. A developmental approach is needed to determine whether disappointed expectations for support play a role in the genesis of marital conflict and even abuse (see Chapter 4, this volume).

Women May Be More
Emotionally Invested in Relationships

A final possibility is that men and women simply have different interpersonal needs. Women may be more emotionally invested in their marriages than men. That is, women may seek to have their emotional needs met in the marriage (i.e., for intimacy, attachment, self-disclosure) and may place a higher value on the adequacy of the marriage to meet such needs (Gove et al., 1983). There is some evidence that the relational schemas of women are more complex and highly developed than those of men (Wong & Czikszintmihalyi, 1991). Thus, women may attend more closely to the behaviors of their spouses. I have found some evidence of greater attentiveness among women to the behaviors of their spouses (Cutrona & Suhr, 1994). Among women, the number of supportive statements made by their husbands during an interaction task was the strongest predictor of the women's satisfaction with the interaction. Among men, however, their overall assessment of their wives' supportiveness before the interaction was a much stronger predictor of satisfaction with the interaction than the actual number of supportive behaviors they received from their wives. For men, a general schema of relationship quality appeared to dominate their evaluation process, whereas for women, the specific behaviors of their spouses were processed and integrated into their interaction evaluations.

✤ The Need for Process Research

Most studies of social support in marriage have been large epidemiological investigations of heterogeneous samples who were assessed at a single point in time as they faced a wide variety of stressful circumstances. There is a need for studies that examine the processes through which husbands and wives deal with specific stressful life circumstances together. There is also a need for studies that examine the ways in which marital partners falter in their attempts to provide support to one another. It would be informative to compare the processes of support exchange in heterosexual couples to those in gay and lesbian couples. Support processes may be different in same-sex couples because both members have been socialized to adopt the same gender role, although in general, societally sanctioned gender roles are less pronounced among gay and lesbian individuals (Kurdek, 1987, 1989).

Research on the process of coping with stress is discussed in the next chapter. To set the stage for such a discussion, I provide below an overview of potential gender differences in the ways that men and women prefer to deal with stress, the effects of differences in coping styles on well-being, and the implications of such differences for intervention.

❧ Gender Differences in Coping

People have their own distinctive ways of coping with problems. A wide variety of factors may influence their typical approach to difficulties, including their gender, their personality, and the way problems were dealt with in their childhood home. People also differ in the kinds of events that affect them emotionally. For example, women react more strongly than men to negative events that occur in the lives of the people they know, for example, a friend's diagnosis of breast cancer or a child's experiences of rejection by peers (Kessler & McLeod, 1985). There is some evidence that men react more strongly than women to problems in the workplace (Folkman & Lazarus, 1980). Thus, a husband may not realize or understand the distress that is experienced by his wife over a friend's misfortune, and she may not comprehend the extent to which a perceived failure at work affects his well-being.

Men and women may also differ in how they think about or appraise negative events in their lives. Appraisals of events may influence the specific course of action chosen to confront problems. Problems appraised as controllable lead to efforts at solution, whereas problems appraised as uncontrollable lead to acceptance or giving up (Folkman & Lazarus, 1980). In one study, women rated events in their daily lives as more severe than did men and more often blamed themselves for their problems (Ptacek, Smith, & Zanas, 1992). In the same study, men rated events in their lives as more expected and controllable than did women. There is evidence that, on average, men appraise themselves as having more control over their lives than do women (Lefcourt, 1981; Pearlin & Schooler, 1978; Wheaton, 1980). Thoits (1991), however, found no differences between women and men in their appraisals of the controllability of events or in the degree of blame they assigned to themselves for their problems. To the extent that men and women do appraise events differently, this may lead to a lack of empathy for the other's feelings. It may also lead to conflict over the strategies chosen to deal with events. For example, a wife may become frustrated over her husband's efforts to control something that she believes must simply be accepted.

The literature on gender-related differences in coping provides some evidence that men and women do approach problems somewhat differently, although the differences are small in magnitude and do not emerge in all studies (Rosario, Shinn, Morch, & Huckabee, 1988; Thoits, 1991). The stereotype is that men approach problems analytically and unemotionally, with a steadfast focus on practical ways to remedy the situation. In the stereotype, women become emotional when they encounter adversity and allow their emotions to interfere with practical problem solving. Dependence on others for help or rescue is also part of the female stereotype.

Men reported greater use of direct problem-solving strategies than did women in two community samples of adults (Pearlin & Schooler, 1978; Stone & Neale, 1984). Studies of younger college student samples do not tend to yield gender differences favoring men in frequency of direct problem solving, however (Ptacek et al., 1992; Rosario et al., 1988; Thoits, 1991). Furthermore, there is some suggestion that both genders use direct problem solving in the life domains in which they have the most expertise and power (Thoits, 1991). Folkman and Lazarus (1980) found that men use more problem-solving strategies in the work domain than women; Menaghan (1982) found that women engage in more direct problem solving than men in the context of marital or family problems. Rosario et al. (1988) reason that differences in direct problem solving

between men and women do not emerge in contexts in which men
and women have equal status and access to resources. Their predictions were confirmed in studies of male and female group therapists
and child care workers at residential treatment facilities for children.
In these settings, men and women were equally likely to use direct
problem solving to cope with problems (Rosario et al., 1988).

Regarding women's greater emotionality in response to stressors,
results are again mixed. Women reported more frequent venting of
emotions than men in a study of middle-aged couples (Stone &
Neale, 1984) and in a study of college undergraduates (Thoits, 1991).
Strategies aimed at reducing the intensity of emotions were reported
with equal frequency in Folkman and Lazarus's (1980) study of
middle-aged community residents and in Ptacek et al.'s (1992) study
of college undergraduates. More frequent use of coping strategies
designed to diminish the intensity of emotions was reported by men
than by women in Rosario et al.'s (1988) study of child care workers.

Men and women tend to use somewhat different strategies for
dealing with their emotions. Men report efforts to control their
emotions through exercise, sports, drinking, and smoking (Rosario
et al., 1988; Thoits, 1991). They also report withdrawal from the
situation more frequently than women (Repetti, 1989; Rosario et al.,
1988). Women more frequently report direct expression of their
feelings through talking to another person or writing about their
emotions (Stone & Neale, 1984; Thoits, 1991).

Perhaps the most consistent gender-related difference in coping
behaviors is the greater tendency of women than men to seek social
support from others. This pattern has been found among undergraduate students, adults, and workplace samples equated for status
and access to resources (Ptacek et al., 1992; Rosario et al., 1988; Stone
& Neale, 1984; Thoits, 1991). Women more frequently seek both
counsel and comfort from others when they are stressed than do men.

In the research summarized above, most differences between men
and women in coping strategies are relatively small and many of the
differences in coping do not emerge consistently across studies.
Differences between people may become more noticeable or significant in times of severe stress, whether the differences are associated
with gender, personality, or past experience. The consequences of
such differences are illustrated in a study of the parents of seriously

ill children conducted by Gottlieb and Wagner (1991). Personal interviews were conducted with 31 parents of children who suffered from either cystic fibrosis or childhood-onset diabetes. In the interviews, marked differences emerged between the reactions of mothers and fathers to their child's illness. The greatest difference appeared in the domain of emotional expression. Mothers frequently expressed intense emotions connected with their child's suffering, worsening of their child's condition, and, above all, fears for their child's future. Fathers remained much more impassive. They rarely verbalized apprehensions about the child's future. They preferred to handle daily problems as they arose, without dwelling on potential catastrophes. Because women assumed most of the responsibility for caregiving, they were immersed in daily experiences of caregiving that included home treatments, blood tests, and insulin injections. They were responsible for preparing special foods, supervising the child's adherence to dietary restrictions, and managing doctor visits, and they witnessed the pain associated with treatment and diagnostic procedures. In contrast, fathers were able to escape from these draining experiences to the workplace, where they reported relief from the strains of their child's illness. Fathers appeared to compartmentalize their lives and were able to derive pleasure from sources of satisfaction outside the family.

Couples in Gottlieb and Wagner's (1991) study described mounting tensions that resulted from these stylistic differences in coping. Husbands accused their wives of emotional overinvolvement. They pressured their wives to behave more "maturely," to engage in less self-pity, and to overdramatize less. They asked to be spared from hearing their wives' fears and apprehensions because such self-disclosures were upsetting to their own equilibrium. They exhorted their wives to focus their energies on the child's needs and simply to accept the rigors of caregiving. Wives accused their husbands of not being involved enough, either emotionally or in the taxing routines of caring for the child. They exerted pressure on their husbands to express their emotions and urged them to assume a greater share of the responsibility for the child's home treatment regimens and general care. Women reported hiding their emotions from their husbands to gain their approval but said they resented the strain this placed on them. In addition, feeling unable to express

their deepest emotions to their husbands led to feelings of isolation
and loneliness among wives.

❧ Conclusions

Studies have documented a variety of gender-related differences,
including the extent to which marriage benefits health, the extent to
which marital quality affects well-being, the amount and quality of
support provided and received, primary sources of support, appraisal of negative life events, and strategies for coping with problems.
It should be emphasized that gender is only one source of differences among people. Personality, experiences in family of origin, and
cultural traditions are examples of other important sources of differences in how people cope individually and jointly with adversity.
Regardless of the source, the way that couples deal with such
stylistic differences can have a profound effect on the success with
which they handle difficult life circumstances. Because of their
interdependence, marital partners are affected not only by the effect
of events on their own emotional well-being but also by the effect
of the stressor on their partners' adjustment and by the methods
their partners use to cope with the strain. Each tries to cope using
long-established patterns of stress management. The coping behaviors of one may be incompatible with the needs of the partner,
however. Adjustments in coping behaviors may be made to win the
other's approval and support, but these adjustments may have
negative consequences, as illustrated by the resentment and loneliness of mothers who hide emotions connected with their child's
illness from their spouses.

The importance of recognizing, understanding, and communicating openly about differences cannot be emphasized enough. With
effort and compassion, marriage partners can benefit from the
balance provided by the other's approach to dealing with crises. Without such efforts, the other's differences may be viewed as a personal
threat and evidence of indifference to the relationship.

3

❦

Giving and Taking Support
A Complicated Process

Jeanette and Mark have been married for 6 years. The first year of their marriage was especially trying because Jeanette, then 29 years old, was diagnosed with a serious illness the month after they returned from their honeymoon. Jeanette tells her memories of that first year:

"I went into the clinic because I thought I was pregnant—my symptoms were really minor, just some changes in my periods. When the doctor told me I had a tumor, I panicked. My mother had just died of cancer 2 years before. I cried and cried. I couldn't wait to see Mark and have him hold me. I guess I believed he could protect me in some way. He didn't say much when I told him, but all the color disappeared from his face. After a few minutes, he started asking me a lot of questions about my exact diagnosis and treatments and prognosis. I didn't know any of the answers. I just knew I was terrified. Later on, when the results of the biopsy came back, we had to decide what kind of treatment I should have. I knew I needed lots of information to make an informed decision. I am a professor, so I headed to the library and did as much research as I could on the specific type of cancer I had. Mark encouraged me in this and read all the articles I brought home from the library. When I wasn't occupied at the library, however, I was really depressed. My prognosis was good, but most of the treatments would make me sterile. I had also seen what chemotherapy had done to my mom—she was always nauseous and she lost so much of her hair that she had to wear a wig. I hated the thought of those poisonous chemicals inside me. I was living in a nightmare. We hadn't been married very long, and I didn't want *to drag Mark down into it. Plus, I really didn't have the words to express how much pain I was in. I went on walks by myself and cried in the bathroom. I remember, one day I walked to the playground near our house. I sat on the top of the jungle gym and cried for the little brown-eyed daughter I would never have. I felt so alone. After a while, I saw Mark coming toward me across the playground. I was so glad to see him. I still didn't know how to tell him what I was feeling, but I was glad that he had known to come after me. He joined me on top of the jungle gym and he put his arm around me. We sat there together until it got dark, hardly talking at all.*

"Over the next weeks and months, Mark frequently told me that he knew I would be okay and that I didn't need to worry. I felt cheated when he said that—I had cancer, for God's sake! Of course I had to worry, and why wasn't he worrying more? I never felt unloved, just annoyed that he didn't acknowledge the seriousness of my situation. In every other way, he knocked himself out to be helpful—cooking, making phone calls for me, trying to minimize the everyday hassles that I had to deal with.

"It was only after the surgery was clearly a success and we found out that I would be able to have children that Mark ever admitted out loud how frightened he had been. He said, 'I just couldn't think about losing you. I couldn't handle it.' I learned a lot about Mark that year—that he deals with some things differently than I do. I also don't take everything he says at face value. I pay more attention to what he does than what he says when times get rough."

Jeanette's story illustrates the complexity of the process that goes on when two people try to cope together with problems in their life. First, coping is an ongoing process. Most problems are not solved quickly, and people go through a variety of phases in their efforts to manage both the situation causing the problem and their own emotional reactions to the situation (Folkman & Lazarus, 1980; Lazarus & Folkman, 1984). Second, as discussed in the previous chapter, people are different in the way they react to problems. In a marriage, difficulties can arise because the husband's and wife's efforts to deal with problems may lead to conflict, misunderstanding, or emotional distance between them (Gottlieb & Wagner, 1991).

Third, traditional measures of social support cannot capture much of what is most important in the unfolding processes through which intimates provide comfort and reassurance to each other. For example, Mark would not have scored high on a measure of frequency of emotionally supportive behaviors—yet Jeanette derived great comfort from the fact that he realized that she needed him the day that her despair was most intense. His behavior had symbolic significance for her that it might not have had for others. Traditional subjective measures of perceived supportiveness may capture the ultimate effect of a partner's behaviors, but they do not yield understanding into the factors that contribute to the behaviors' effectiveness or lack of effectiveness.

In efforts to understand the processes through which marital partners cope jointly with stress, it is important to consider the personalities and prior experiences of both partners that contribute to their willingness to confide in one another, their evaluation of their partners' support-intended behaviors, and their willingness to accept comfort or advice from their spouses. Perhaps even more important are characteristics of the relationship. Is this a relationship of trust, open communication, and mutual appreciation or one of formality, distrust, and resentment? The relationship context in which people attempt to cope with negative events is a critical determinant of the success with which couples deal individually and jointly with crises.

Three stages of the social support process are described in this chapter. Factors that facilitate or hinder couples' successful negotiation of adverse circumstances are considered at each of these stages.

Based on intensive interviews with couples about how they deal with employment-related stresses, both individually and with their partners, Pearlin and McCall (1990) describe three stages of interactive coping. The first stage involves revelation of the problem to the partner. In the second stage, the partner appraises the situation to determine whether support is necessary, appropriate, or likely to be successful and whether or not he or she is willing to provide it. The third stage includes actual support-intended transactions, some of which have the effect of providing comfort or mobilizing an effective response to the problem and some of which generate disappointment, resentment, or further demoralization. Each stage can proceed smoothly or go awry, and the manner in which each is navigated has important implications for the success or failure of the next phase. Each phase is described below, along with research findings that are relevant to the processes that transpire in each. Factors that promote mutually satisfying outcomes and factors that frustrate such outcomes are highlighted.

❧ Revelation of the Problem

The stress victim must decide whether or not to disclose a stressful event or problem to his or her partner, unless the event has occurred in a shared domain (e.g., one of the children is sick). A variety of factors may influence this decision, including the personality of the stressed individual, the nature of the relationship between the marital partners, and expectations about the partner's reaction to disclosure of the problem (Barbee et al., 1993; Pearlin & McCall, 1990).

Personality and Disclosure

A range of personality factors may influence the decision of whether or not to disclose stressful events to the spouse. In Pearlin and McCall's (1990) sample, some people expressed a strong need for privacy and a belief that certain kinds of experiences simply should not be discussed with others, even an intimate partner. Others expressed belief in the importance of self-sufficiency, that one should not rely on others for assistance. Individual differences in willingness to use social support contribute to the amount of social support received (Eckenrode, 1983; Vaux, Burda, & Stewart, 1986). Those who are comfortable with and value support from others receive higher levels of support from others.

Barbee et al. (1993) speculate about the role of attachment style as a determinant of whether or not marital partners turn to each other for assistance. Research by Simpson, Rholes, and Nelligan (1992) reveals that women with a secure attachment style are more likely to seek support when they experience anxiety than those with a more anxious attachment style. Individuals whose early life experiences portrayed other people as unreliable, uncaring, or even hostile are less likely to entrust others with their private worries and concerns than those whose experiences were characterized by caring and accessible others.

The Relationship Context

Issues in the relationship can also affect the decision of whether or not to disclose a current difficulty to one's mate. Several such issues are described by Pearlin and McCall (1990). Wishing to protect a partner who is already overburdened with worries may lead an individual to keep a problem to herself or himself. For example, an individual may fear that news of impending layoffs at work will lead the spouse to panic over the financial implications of job loss for the family. Reluctance to deal with the partner's emotional reaction to the problem may also inhibit self-disclosure: "If I told him what happened, he'd be furious. I'd have to put all my energy into calming him down and keeping him from doing something that would make the situation worse than it already is." Sometimes, people fear that disclosure of a stressor will lead to conflict. For example, the situation causing distress may have been one that the partner advised against becoming involved in: "I told you that was a stupid investment. I just knew John wasn't a good businessman." The problem situation may involve other "hot" themes in the relationship, such as jealousy or time spent away from home: "I don't care when that grant is due. I refuse to spend another weekend alone!"

Past experiences in which the partner's efforts to provide support were aversive or unsatisfactory may also cause a person to keep a problem to herself or himself. Unwanted advice is particularly troublesome: "Every time I tell him about a problem, he gives me a lecture about what I should do. It makes me mad, because he doesn't know anything about the situation. He's never dealt with those people. But he keeps after me—'Did you tell him you'll quit if you don't get that raise?' "

Delaying Disclosure

Sometimes, individuals decide to wait before disclosing a problem to their mate. Pearlin and McCall (1990) describe several reasons for the decision to delay communicating a problem to one's spouse. People sometimes do not know exactly what is bothering them about a situation and want to figure out why they are upset before sharing these feelings with their spouses. Individuals may want to "cool off" before disclosing an event to their partners to gain control over strong emotions. Finally, some individuals want to make some progress toward solving the problem before discussing it with their mate. Both of the latter situations may be construed as "face-saving" strategies, motivated by a reluctance for one's partner to see one as "out of control"—over either emotions or the stress-producing situation. In the Pearlin and McCall study, this kind of face-saving strategy was used primarily by men.

Consequences of Nondisclosure

There are often negative consequences of failing to disclose a significant stressful event to one's spouse. Although the partner may not know why the individual is upset, behavioral signs of distress, such as irritability, impatience, withdrawal, or preoccupation, are usually noticed (Pearlin & McCall, 1990). Commenting on the person's "bad mood" is often counterproductive: "Get off my back! If I wanted to talk about it, I would—just leave me alone!" The causal attributions made by the partner for the stressed person's ill temper are an important determinant of how he or she reacts. For example, if a wife believes that her husband's withdrawn behavior means that he is angry at her, she may react with guilt and distress. If the wife believes that such anger is unjustified, she may become angry. Alternatively, the wife may guess that something bad must have happened at work for her husband to behave in such an unpleasant or unhappy manner. If past experience suggests that leaving her husband alone will eventually lead to disclosure, difficulties may not develop. The situation may deteriorate into hostility and accusations, however. In the interviews conducted by Pearlin and McCall (1990), some couples said it took a quarrel over nondisclosure for the real problem to come out into the open.

Support Activation Strategies

The manner in which stressed individuals communicate their distress is an important determinant of the quality of response they receive from their spouses. Barbee et al. (1993) refer to people's efforts to solicit support from one another as *support activation strategies*. Support activation strategies may be direct or indirect, verbal or nonverbal. In Barbee et al.'s categorization scheme, a direct verbal strategy is a simple request for support: "Would you make dinner tonight? If I don't finish this report tonight, I'll be behind all week." Indirect verbal strategies include hinting at problems or complaining: "Why do I have to do all the cooking?" In the nonverbal category, Barbee et al. describe direct expression of distress—for example, crying—and indirect expression of distress—such as pouting, sulking, or fidgeting.

My research (Cutrona, Suhr, et al., 1990) suggests that married couples use two specific support activation strategies most frequently. We asked married men and women what they would do or say to elicit social support from their partners in each of a number of different stressful situations (e.g., trouble at work, problems with a friend). For both men and women, the most frequent response was, "I would just tell him (her) what happened." This is less direct than specifying that support is required—"Will you help me?"—or describing the specific support behavior that is sought—"Tell me you think I'll do a good job tomorrow." Subjects clearly believed that describing a stressful situation to their partners implied that a supportive response was desired. When they did not describe the problem situation to their partners, individuals frequently disclosed their emotional state—either verbally or nonverbally. A description of the emotion—"I'm really bummed out"—was viewed as an implied request for the spouse to inquire about the reason for feeling unhappy.

A number of factors may influence the type of support activation strategies that people use. Barbee et al. (1993) summarize several of these factors, including gender, social skill level, and personality. As noted above, women are more likely to seek social support in times of stress than men (Rosario et al., 1988). Women's greater comfort with asking for support may lead them to use direct strategies more often than men do. Belle (1987) found that women are indeed more likely than men to express openly their need for support. On the average, women have a higher level of social skill than men (Sarason et al., 1985), which may allow them to express their support needs more clearly. In our research (Cutrona, Suhr, et al., 1990), however, we found that the one support activation strategy that was used significantly more frequently by women than by men was an indirect strategy—a description or display of the emotion that was triggered by the stressor.

Problems Communicating the Need for Support

Indirect support activation strategies are harder to interpret than either direct requests for assistance or clear-cut expressions of distress. Because they are harder to read, they are often misinterpreted. As described previously, the partner's attributions for the stressed individual's behavior may lead to patient tolerance, worry over having caused offense, or a major blowup. Barbee et al. (1993) describe a variety of problems that may result from the use of indirect support activation strategies. Even if an indirect solicitation strategy is correctly read as a sign that the partner wants or needs support, the type of support desired may not be understood. Complaining may lead to advice—"Well, tell your boss you just can't finish the report in one day"—when relief from time-consuming chores was what was actually desired—"If you'd do the dishes and put the kids to bed tonight, I think I could get a draft of my final report done by the deadline."

Indirect activation behaviors may be perceived as manipulative: "If you wanted me to make dinner, why didn't you just say so, instead of laying a guilt trip on me." Some strategies may be intrinsically aversive to their target, such as whining or crying, and may lead the partner to criticize or withdraw. Using such strategies places the stressed individual at a disadvantage, because she or he has generated annoyance or distaste in the partner rather than empathy (Barbee et al., 1993).

In contrast, when the stressed person delivers a clear support activation message and the partner understands the message and responds appropriately, the rewards for both can be significant. As described by Barbee et al. (1993), the stressed person feels understood and cared for. The helper is gratified by the response of the stressed person and experiences self-efficacy and pride. As mentioned in Chapter 1, over time such exchanges are vitally important to the creation of trust.

❧ Appraisal of Support Needs by the Partner

Once the partner is aware that his or her spouse is facing a stressor, the partner must decide what, if anything to do about it. In Pearlin and McCall's (1990) study of work stress, the most frequent response to the revelation that the spouse was facing difficulties at work was to provide support of some kind. In my observational studies of married couples (Cutrona & Suhr, 1992), spouses all provided at least one supportive behavior to their partners within 10 minutes of learning that he or she was facing a stressful situation; the average number of supportive behaviors was 17.5 in the 10-minute observation period.

Support Is Not Always Provided

There are certainly circumstances in which husbands and wives do not attempt to help each other even when they know help is desired. Several such circumstances are described by Pearlin and McCall (1990). The stressed person's problem may not be evaluated as legitimate or of sufficient magnitude to merit assistance by the spouse: "Why are you so upset over the way she talked to you? She can't do anything to you. Why do you even care?" In the context of other problems facing the family, the stressed person's complaints may not appear to merit the allocation of resources or effort: "Your son may need surgery this month! How can you even think of sending money to your sister?"

The partner's beliefs about the causes of the situation causing stress are also relevant to decisions about whether or not to offer support. Weiner (1980) documents that when people believe that the cause of another's plight is out of that person's control (e.g., becoming ill and falling down), they feel pity and are likely to offer assistance. When people believe that the cause of another's misfortune was within that person's control (e.g., getting drunk and falling down), however, they feel revulsion or anger and are less likely to offer assistance. Within couples, help from the spouse may be more likely when the spouse believes that the stressor was not something that could have been prevented. If the spouse believes that the stressor could have been prevented and blames the situation on the individual seeking support, help is unlikely to be forthcoming.

The partner's emotional state may also play a key role in his or her reaction to a request for support. A series of studies by Barbee and her colleagues documents that people are more likely to use effective social support strategies when they are in a positive mood than when they are in a negative mood. For example, when a sad mood was experimentally induced, people did not recognize the need to provide support or seemed to lack the energy to provide it (Barbee, 1990b, 1991; Yankeelov, Barbee, Cunningham, & Druen, 1991). In my observational studies of married couples (Cutrona & Suhr, 1994), level of depressed mood in the support provider negatively predicted the number of support behaviors individuals provided to their mate.

When a stressful situation lasts for a long time, the resources of the support provider may become depleted and it may not be psychologically or physically possible for that person to provide some kinds of support any longer. Chesler and Barbarin (1984) describe the complex dynamics that arose in couples who were the parents of a chronically ill child. Husbands were ambivalent about responding to their wives' expressions of distress. They reported feeling drained of resources, deprived of support from their unhappy wives, and uncertain how to elicit support for their own emotional needs. In Chapter 5, the support dynamics of one particular kind of chronic stress are discussed in depth—the problems that arise when one member of the couple is chronically ill.

Problems that have arisen frequently in the past may lead to a sense of futility in the support provider, whose previous efforts to provide assistance did not prove successful or were not appreciated by the stressed spouse: "I know what you're going to say. You think your boss is playing favorites and leaving you out of decisions. Every time this comes up, I tell you to apply for a transfer, but you seem to want to keep beating your head against the wall! There's nothing more I can say."

When the stressed partner becomes clinically depressed, a number of difficulties arise (Barbee et al., 1993). Prolonged distress may lead to loss of patience in the nondepressed spouse, who cannot understand why the depressed partner can't "shake it off." The nondepressed partner may be hurt and angered by the depressed partner's irritability, lack of responsivity to helping efforts, and withdrawal from family activities. Previous unsuccessful efforts to cheer or comfort the partner may have led to a feeling of futility (Coyne, Wortman, & Lehman, 1988). There is a consistent body of literature that documents the relation between depression and marital problems. Although marital problems undoubtedly cause depression, it is also true that depression plays a causal role in marital distress (Coyne & Downey, 1991; Gotlib & McCabe, 1990).

Relationship Issues and
Willingness to Provide Support

Long-standing issues in the relationship can also influence the decision of whether or not to respond to a partner's desire for support. Dunkel-Schetter and Bennett (1990) found that the perception of inequity in support provision caused givers to become less helpful. If one partner is consistently "stuck" in the role of support provider, he or she may become resentful: "Will it ever be my turn to get some sympathy? You're always complaining about how hard it is to work at a crummy job. You think my job is so great? You don't know what I have to put up with!"

A strong negative correlation has been found between conflict and perceived supportiveness in intimate relationships (Abbey, Abramis, & Caplan, 1985). When people are angry at each other, they are less likely to provide support. Thus, if a negative event occurs in the life of one member of a couple during a particularly stormy time in the relationship, that person will receive less support than if the event had happened before the conflict developed. A relationship characterized by frequent and intense conflict is unlikely to be supportive, especially if conflicts go unresolved for long periods of time. Failure to receive support in times of need can be very damaging to a person's relational schema, especially in regard to whether or not the partner can be trusted to provide care when needed. If the spouse can rise above his or her current grievances, set aside angry feelings, and provide support to the needy partner, the stressed individual may be doubly appreciative. Support that is given at personal cost to the provider is especially powerful in the development of trust

(Holmes & Rempel, 1989). Chapter 4 addresses the interplay between conflict and social support in intimate relationships in
more depth.

Finally, in some situations, the spouse may be the source of
distress: "You've been so distant lately. I feel totally rejected and
alone. I don't know what in the world I've done to make you so
angry!" Unless the partner is ready to reconcile, such a disclosure
may lead to greater withdrawal, accusations, or attack. Little is
known about the processes of social support exchange when the
behavior of one spouse is the problem causing unhappiness in the
other. It is difficult to provide support to another when that person
is complaining about one's own behavior. The urge to defend oneself and justify one's actions is likely to prevent the provision of
comfort or assistance. If an individual can swallow his or her pride
and provide support under such circumstances, the behavior may
be an especially salient demonstration that he or she can be relied
on in times of need: "I don't like to admit it, but you're right. I know
I need to see a doctor to find out if anything serious is wrong. It was
easier to think about how mad I was at you for pushing me to make
an appointment than to face the problem. You must have felt really
alone, worrying about me and having me blow up at you every time
you brought up the subject."

ം Providing Support:
What Determines Success?

All attempts to provide support are not successful. Sometimes
well-intentioned efforts to help a loved one lead to resentment,
distress, or alienation rather than to gratitude or comfort (Lehman,
Ellard, & Wortman, 1986). Much remains unknown about the determinants of perceived supportiveness, but research has revealed
some critical dimensions of successful support interactions. These
include the extent to which the support reflects accurate understanding of the problem by the support provider, attributions made
by the recipient regarding why support was given, the manner in
which support is offered (e.g., tone of voice and other nonverbal cues),
the extent to which the support provided matches the type of support

desired, and the extent to which the support provided meets the particular needs engendered by the stressful circumstances.

Support that urges a quick or simple solution to a complex problem is not perceived as helpful because the proposal of such a solution means that the support provider has not fully grasped the situation (Pearlin & McCall, 1990). A perceived lack of empathic understanding is associated with less positive outcomes of psychotherapy (Rogers, 1942), and the same is probably true of informal help-intended interactions.

Support that is provided spontaneously is valued more highly than support that is provided only after a specific request (Cutrona, Cohen, & Igram, 1990). Cutrona, Cohen, et al. (1990) hypothesize that spontaneously provided support is attributed to genuine caring and a desire to help, whereas support provided after an explicit request is more likely to be attributed to duty or compliance. Whenever an external explanation for a supportive behavior is available, the recipient is less likely to attribute support to enduring positive attributes of the giver (Kelley, 1973). Examples of such external factors include the presence of an audience that will be favorably impressed by a supportive response (e.g., parents or friends of the stressed partner) and the availability of external rewards for providing support: "He thinks that if he's nice to me today, I'll forget how mean he was last night." Internal attributions to positive aspects of the provider are more likely when there is no apparent personal benefit to the provider for behaving in a helpful way.

The manner in which a support-intended message is communicated is also an important determinant of its effect. If the provider resents being asked or feels some reluctance to provide assistance, this will most likely come out in his or her tone of voice or body language and will render the support behavior less effective (Leatham & Duck, 1990). Consider the effect of two different responses to a request for help with child care: "OK! OK! I'll change his diapers so you can keep studying. Don't say I never did anything for you!" and "Sure, I'll change the baby. Why don't I take her upstairs for a couple of hours so you can concentrate better on your work." Attributional processes are probably a key component of reactions to assistance that is provided resentfully or reluctantly. Reluctance to provide assistance may trigger an attribution to a lack of caring or an enduring negative trait, such as selfishness or insensitivity (Fincham & Bradbury, 1990).

Disappointed Expectations

Support expectations and the consequences of disappointed expectations have not been extensively studied. Evidence that support expectations play an important role in marital relations comes from research by Ruble (1988). In a study of the transition to parenthood, Ruble found that the difference between the amount of help with child care women expected to receive from their husbands before delivery and the amount of help they actually received was a strong predictor of postpartum distress—stronger than absolute level of child care assistance from the spouse.

Cutrona, Cohen, et al. (1990) found that support is evaluated less positively when it differs in type from that desired by the stressed individual. For example, when comfort is desired but tangible assistance is provided, support is evaluated much more negatively than when comfort is both desired and provided. An unexpected finding from the Cutrona, Cohen, et al. study is that when tangible assistance is desired, emotional support is evaluated almost as positively as the desired tangible support. It appears that tangible assistance cannot substitute when emotional support is desired, but emotional support is viewed as an acceptable substitute for tangible assistance, at least under certain circumstances. In other words, when a hug is wanted, offering to wash the car will not suffice; but when a clean car is wanted, a hug just might do the trick! As is discussed in a later section, emotional support—expressions of caring, empathy, and concern—appears to be valued more highly than any other kind of support, across a wide range of situations.

Optimal Matching of Stressor and Support

Different kinds of stressful events pose different demands. Thus, it makes sense that different kinds of social support are most helpful in the context of different kinds of stressful circumstances (e.g., death of a parent versus receiving a poor evaluation at work). Several researchers have proposed models of optimal matching between stress and support type, but to date, relatively little empirical work has been conducted to test these models. Cohen and McKay (1984) hypothesize that the source of a person's distress plays a major role in the type of support from which he or she benefits maximally. For example, if a resource deficit is the source of stress (e.g., not enough money to pay bills, lack of reliable transportation), then tangible support (loaning money or offering to drive the person to his or her destination) is most useful. If the source of distress is self-blame for perceived personal failure (e.g., a poor grade on a term paper), however, then esteem support will be of greatest use: "You were sick all week, and I know you weren't satisfied with how much time you could put into studying. You can make up for it on the final exam." If an exaggerated assessment of the seriousness of the situation is at the source of the person's distress, appraisal support that helps the person put the situation in perspective will provide the greatest benefit: "It doesn't mean you're going to get fired, just because the boss was crabby with you. She probably had a fight with her husband before work and just took it out on you."

Thoits (1986) divides events broadly into those that impose coping demands for appraisal, problem solution, and emotion management and argues that only social support that facilitates the appropriate coping responses should be effective.

Cohen and Wills (1985) argue that some kinds of social support are beneficial across a wide range of circumstances but others are useful only when they address a specific loss or deficit. On the basis of an extensive review of the literature, Cohen and Wills conclude that informational support (advice and factual input) and esteem support (encouragement and recognition of competence) are helpful in virtually all situations but that tangible support is beneficial only when the stress has led to a need for materials or assistance (e.g., the person has a flat tire or needs a baby-sitter during a doctor's appointment). Similarly, social integration or belonging support is most beneficial in the context of a stress that involves the loss of one or more relationships (e.g., moving to a new community).

My work has emphasized the controllability of events as a key determinant of the type of support that is most beneficial (Cutrona, 1990; Cutrona & Russell, 1990; Cutrona & Suhr, 1992). Building on the work of Lazarus and Folkman (1984), I have hypothesized that when facing events that are potentially controllable—that is, there is something the person (or the supporter) can do to prevent the event or diminish its severity—the most appropriate type of support provides assistance or resources for direct action to solve the problem. By contrast, when facing events that are uncontrollable—that is, there is nothing the person or the supporter can do to prevent the event or diminish its severity—the most appropriate type of support provides comfort (i.e., expressions of caring and concern).

I have tested this model with married couples (Cutrona & Suhr, 1992). Couples were asked to think of a source of current distress and to disclose this stress to their spouses. The spouse was instructed to react spontaneously to this disclosure. At the end of 10 minutes, the conversations were terminated and the stressed person rated the supportiveness of his or her partner's behaviors during the interaction. The conversations, which were videotaped, were later coded. Trained observers rated the controllability of each stress that was disclosed, both with respect to its controllability by the discloser and its controllability by the spouse (i.e., was there anything the spouse could do to prevent the negative event or ease its severity?). A different set of observers coded the number and type of support behaviors that were provided by the spouse during the disclosure session. The frequency of five different types of support was tallied using the Social Support Behavior Code (SSBC) (Cutrona & Suhr, 1992; Suhr, 1990). A single type of support varied in its effectiveness as a function of the controllability of the stress under discussion. This type was informational support. When spouses had a high degree of potential control over the discloser's stressful circumstances, the more advice and guidance they provided, the more supportive they were rated by the discloser. When disclosers had a high degree of potential control over their own stressful circumstances, the more advice and guidance they received from their spouses, the less supportive they rated their spouses' behavior during the interaction. For example, a colleague revealed that she frequently asks her statistician husband to look over her manuscripts to make sure that the statistical analyses were conducted and are described correctly. She is grateful for this assistance and does not resent suggestions. The same colleague considers herself quite expert at writing and complains that her husband criticizes her grammar when he reads her manuscripts. She resents this input and has considered finding another statistician to read her papers.

Thus, it appears that informational support is welcome only when the person providing it has resources or expertise that are directly relevant to the problem and when the stressed person lacks such resources or expertise. By contrast, one type of support was uniformly received positively across both high- and low-control events—emotional support. Expressions of caring and concern were associated with high levels of perceived support across all kinds of stressful event disclosures. The message seems to be, "When in doubt, provide emotional support!"

⚜ Conclusions

A complex series of steps is involved in the process of providing and receiving social support in the context of intimate relationships. One determinant of how smoothly the process proceeds is the communication skills of the participants. The stress victim must be able to communicate his or her need for support in a way that delivers a clear message and motivates the spouse to make an effort to meet his or her needs. It is useful to have a broad repertoire of support elicitation strategies. If initial attempts are not successful in soliciting support, the stress victim can then switch to a second strategy. For example, if an indirect strategy (sighing and looking crestfallen) does not elicit support, a more direct strategy (describing the distressing event) may succeed. If the partner delivers an unwanted type of support, it may be necessary for the stressed individual to request the desired support explicitly: "Just hold me and tell me it'll be OK." Skill at identifying and communicating personal needs is critical for the individual seeking social support.

For the support provider, the ability to interpret accurately both verbal and nonverbal messages from the partner is important. Formulating questions that will yield clarification of the message that the stress victim is sending requires skill because individuals often assume that their partners "should know" what they are feeling and what they need: "I shouldn't have to tell you—if you really loved me, you'd know what to do!" Alas, we do not always know what our loved ones want, and it is good to have a wide repertoire of supportive behaviors. If advice is not welcomed by the spouse, sympathetic listening or encouragement may ease the partner's distress.

At every stage in the support process, individuals make causal attributions for their partners' behavior—that is, they try to explain why the partner behaved as he or she did. The causal explanations that people generate for their partners' behavior at each stage of the support process can determine whether warm, caring emotions or hurt, resentful feelings are evoked. Attributions for disclosure or failure to disclose a hurtful incident, providing or withholding support, providing a particular kind of support—all can have significant consequences. A complex combination of personal, situational, and relationship factors enters into causal attributions for the behavior of one's spouse. As noted previously, however, once a schema of high trust has been developed, even negative spouse behaviors are likely to be assimilated into an overall positive picture of the partner (Holmes & Rempel, 1989). Vigilance relaxes and good intentions are consistently attributed to the partner. A consistent history of supportive exchanges between partners encourages the development of a trusting relationship, especially when support is provided at personal cost or in the absence of external reinforcement. The relationship is less vulnerable to disruption once a high level of trust has been established because partners no longer need frequent proof of their partners' commitment and goodwill.

The emotional tone of a relationship influences how smoothly members of a couple deal with stressful life events. If a person fears rejection or ridicule, he or she will find it difficult to confide feelings of vulnerability. If an individual is angry at his or her partner, even the most skillfully worded support elicitation will not yield a supportive response. If the appropriate or desired type of assistance is given in a manner that communicates scorn or disdain, it will not provide comfort. The give-and-take of social support is strongly influenced by other events in the emotional history and current life of the relationship. It is impossible to understand the flow of positive behaviors in a relationship without some knowledge of the negatives. Similarly, it is not possible to understand the genesis of negative behaviors without knowledge of the positives that have or have not been provided. The interplay of conflict and social support is examined in depth in the following chapter.

The ongoing dynamics that facilitate the provision of sensitively timed and worded support are not well understood. More research is needed on what transpires in naturally occurring support trans-actions. Although a rich and informative literature has accumulated on the dynamics of marital conflict, much less is known about those of marital support. A better understanding of marital support transactions is needed because their facilitation should be a key component of marital preparation interventions and interventions designed to alleviate marital distress.

4

The Interplay Between
Conflict and Social Support
Do Positive
Behaviors Really Matter?

Karen and Rick had been married for 3 years when they received the news that Karen's mother had terminal cancer. The news came at a time when both Karen and Rick were under considerable stress from other sources: Karen was a first-year graduate student and Rick was in the first year of his residency in internal medicine at an urban hospital. They filed for divorce 2 years later. Karen feels that the stress of her mother's illness played a major role in the deterioration of the relationship. She tells her side of the story:

"I think we were both pretty immature when we got married. We'd been protected by our families and had never had to face real adversity. I think that my mother's illness scared us both. We both wanted to run for cover. Rick was overwhelmed by the responsibilities of being a real doctor for the first time, and he hated coming home to my worries over my mom. He said that he dealt with sickness and death all day and he couldn't handle getting involved emotionally in my mother's illness. His attitude made me mad, but I made a real effort not to burden him. I didn't talk about my emotions at

AUTHOR'S NOTE: Portions of this chapter also appear in Cutrona (1996). Reprinted with permission of Plenum.

all. I tried to be matter-of-fact when I reported the latest developments in my mom's condition. We didn't talk about his experiences at the hospital much either. As I look back, it's clear that we were both pretty self-centered. Neither of us really reached out to help the other. I was so mad at him for not helping me deal with my misery that I resented every little thing he did wrong. He started staying at the hospital later and later—sometimes staying away all night even when he wasn't on call. I started relying on my friends in graduate school for emotional support. During the 2 years my mother lived after diagnosis, my family really pulled together, and I became closer to both my parents and my brother. But Rick and I were never really close again. We had shut away such important parts of ourselves from each other. There was just nothing to hold us together."

In close relationships, negative behaviors, such as criticism, sarcasm, and belittling, appear to have more effect on morale and relationship satisfaction than do positive behaviors, including social support (Barrera, 1981; Fiore, Becker, & Coppel, 1983; Kiecolt-Glaser, Dyer, & Shuttleworth, 1988; Rook, 1984b; Schuster, Kessler, & Aseltine, 1990; Vinokur & van Ryn, 1993). Why then is it worthwhile to pursue the study of social support within marriage? Would it be more fruitful to abandon the study of help-intended behaviors between husbands and wives and concentrate exclusively on ways to curb destructive interactions?

An exclusive focus on hurtful and uncooperative behavior within couples would be a serious mistake. In this chapter, I argue that the quality and probability of survival of marital relationships can be significantly affected by the frequency and sensitivity of supportive acts exchanged by husbands and wives. Support within the marital relationship can promote a positive emotional tone and prevent the acceleration of negative interactions that cause relationship deterioration. Support also can foster intimacy and closeness that hold couples together through difficult times. As illustrated in the example above, a lack of support can accelerate negative interactions and erode the love that individuals feel for one another.

Four different mechanisms through which social support may contribute to the quality and survival of marital relationships are described in this chapter. First, during times of severe stress, support from the spouse can prevent emotional withdrawal and isolation that can damage the relationship. Second, during times of stress, support from the spouse can prevent the onset of clinically significant depression and the aversive behaviors associated with depression that are damaging to relationships (e.g., self-pity, irritability, loss of sex drive). Third, in the context of the inevitable disagreements that arise between couples, supportlike behaviors can prevent conflicts from escalating in intensity to the point where they become destructive. Fourth, self-disclosure and emotional intimacy are facilitated by supportive communications. Intimate interactions promote a sense of bonding and trust that can ease couples through potentially difficult circumstances. When the partner behaves in an unpleasant or inconsiderate way, attributions for his or her behavior are likely to be more benign when the relationship is characterized by trust and goodwill (Bradbury & Fincham, 1992; Fincham & Bradbury, 1990; Holmes & Rempel, 1989). These benign attributions—"He's really feeling stressed right now"—prevent the occurrence of major blowups over minor transgressions. I summarize evidence in the literature for these four mechanisms in the first part of this chapter.

In the second section of the chapter, I shift focus to mechanisms through which inadequate social support can increase conflict and dissatisfaction with marriage. The effects of perceived and actual inequity in the provision of social support and disappointed expectations for social support are examined. Preliminary data from an observational study of married couples that bear on the interplay of conflict and supportive behaviors in ongoing relationships are described.

❧ The Role of Social Support in Relationship Maintenance

Preventing Stress-Related Deterioration

Under conditions of high stress (e.g., financial problems, death of a family member, serious illness), any marriage can show signs of distress. Compared to nonclinic couples, couples who seek marital counseling report almost twice the frequency of stressful life events in the 3 years prior to initiating treatment and a significant increase in stress the year immediately preceding treatment initiation (Bird, Schuham, Benson, & Gans, 1981). Even psychologically "healthy" individuals can experience marital deterioration following stressful life events. Susceptibility to marital problems following negative life events is not limited to those who have a lifelong history of problems coping with stress. Couples who seek help for marital problems often score within the normal range on measures of neuroticism and other indices of adjustment (Libman, Takefman, & Brender, 1980).

Marital deterioration is not inevitable following adverse life events. Variability in the effect of traumatic events on the marital relationship can be illustrated by the inconsistent results found in the bereavement literature. Some studies indicate that following the death of a child, marital stability is seriously diminished (Helmrath & Steinitz, 1978; Levav, 1982). High rates of marital breakup are reported by some authors following childhood cancer fatalities (Kaplan, Smith, Grobstein, & Fischman, 1973) and after the sudden death of a child by drowning (Nixon & Pearn, 1977). Conversely, a number of studies indicate that marital problems and divorces are not disproportionately common following tragic events in the family. No increases in marital instability were found in several studies of couples whose child died of cancer (Lansky, Cairns, Hassanein, Wehr, & Lowman, 1978; Oakley & Patterson, 1966; Stehbens & Lascari, 1974). The death or serious illness of a family member may actually enhance communication and closeness among surviving members (Koch, 1985; McCubbin & Patterson, 1983; Shanfield & Swain, 1984).

In the view of Lehman and colleagues, marital relationships appear to polarize following tragedy—they either significantly worsen or significantly improve (Lehman, Lang, Wortman, & Sorenson, 1989). Lehman et al. (1989) found significantly more divorces or separations among couples who suffered the loss of a child within the previous 4 to 7 years compared to nonbereaved controls. Responses to the question "How do you feel your child's death affected your marriage?" however, were fairly evenly divided between those who felt their marriage had been weakened and those who felt it had been strengthened. Of the bereaved parents, 21% reported that after their child's death their marriage became somewhat or much worse; 29% reported that it become somewhat or much better.

In the Lehman et al. (1989) study, a common theme among parents whose marriages deteriorated following the death of a child was that one or both of the bereaved parents withdrew into their own private suffering rather than mourning together. Such withdrawal leaves each parent to cope individually with pain, anger, and grief. Emotional withdrawal, especially when it is more pronounced in one partner than the other, can lead to hurt, confusion, and resentment in the partner who desires more emotional contact (Christensen, 1988; Gottman & Levenson, 1985; Jacobson & Margolin, 1979). A pattern of emotional pursuit and flight may develop in which both partners become increasingly frustrated and angry.

It has been hypothesized that one mechanism through which marriage bestows its protective mental health function is by promoting a joint identity, a way of thinking of oneself as part of a whole (Gove et al., 1983). Loss of this joint identity may be most likely during times of severe stress (Russell, 1988). Couples who are able to provide support to one another during times of duress may be able to prevent emotional withdrawal. If highly stressed partners can maintain emotional contact with one another and weather adverse circumstances as part of a whole rather than in emotional isolation, their relationship may sustain less damage. Sensitive and well-timed support from the spouse is an important component of maintaining emotional contact and reducing emotional isolation. When a stressor affects both parties emotionally, successful couples may adopt a strategy of "turn taking," in which the individual who is momentarily most needy receives comfort from the other, who is secure in the knowledge that when his or her emotions become overwhelming, comfort will be forthcoming from the partner.

Preventing Clinical Depression

A second mechanism through which social support may prevent relationship deterioration in times of duress is through its effect on individual well-being. Distress may be less likely to turn into clinically significant depression if spousal support is available (Brown & Harris, 1978). The irritability, self-involvement, lack of motivation, and intense dysphoria that characterize prolonged clinical depression become highly aversive to spouse, family, and friends over time. A clear link between depression and marital distress has been documented (Coyne & Downey, 1991). Although sometimes marital problems play a causal role in depression, depression often appears to be a causal factor in marital problems (Coyne & Downey, 1991). If sensitive and readily available support from the spouse is forthcoming, in the context of both major calamities and minor setbacks, the onset of clinical depression, with its damaging effects on relationships, may be avoided (Brown & Harris, 1978).

Reducing the Intensity of Conflict

Relationships can break down at a variety of levels from a variety of causes. These include decreased liking for the partner, reduced satisfaction with the partner relative to other potential partners, unsatisfactory performance by the partner of role obligations, sexual problems, differences in desired intimacy, and dissatisfaction with the relative rewards and costs of maintaining the relationship (Duck, 1981). Contributing to many of these problems are skill deficits on the part of one or both partners (Jacobson & Margolin, 1979). A survey of marital therapists revealed that poor communication was far and away the problem that therapists felt was most damaging to relationships (Geiss & O'Leary, 1981).

A number of researchers have compared the communication behaviors of distressed versus nondistressed couples. A pattern of consistent differences has emerged. Compared to nondistressed couples, distressed couples display more negative affect (negative tone of voice, nonverbal inattention), more negative verbal behaviors (criticism, disagreement, sarcasm), less positive affect (smiling, positive tone of voice), and fewer positive verbal behaviors (approval, agreement, support) (Birchler, Weiss, & Vincent, 1975; Gottman, 1979; Margolin & Wampold, 1981; Raush, Barry, Hertel, & Swain, 1974; Revenstorf, Vogel, Wegener, Hahlweg, & Schindler, 1980). In addition, individuals in distressed marriages are more likely to reciprocate negative behaviors than those in nondistressed marriages (Gottman, 1979; Margolin & Wampold, 1981). That is, if one partner makes a negative statement, such as a criticism or complaint, there is a very high probability that the spouse will respond with a second negative behavior, such as whining, shouting, or complaining.

One effect of this pattern of negative reciprocation is an increasing spiral of emotional intensity in the conflicts of distressed couples (Gottman, Markman, & Notarius, 1977; Revenstorf et al., 1980). One reason that emotional intensity increases is that couples move from the original topic of disagreement (e.g., who should vacuum the rug) to an exchange of insults and accusations regarding the other's flaws (Raush et al., 1974). Kelley (1979) refers to this as escalation to the *dispositional level*, in which the personal inadequacies and undesirable dispositions of the other are highlighted rather than specific actions or issues. For example, the argument over vacuuming may escalate to a heated exchange of accusations over irresponsibility, slovenliness, and exploitation: "If you weren't such a spoiled brat, you wouldn't treat me like your slave, and you'd help out around here more than once a year!" According to Deutsch (1969), the hallmark of destructive conflict is this escalation, in which the conflict becomes independent of the original issues. Some conflicts may go beyond the "point of no return" in their bitterness and hurtfulness, such that the relationship is never again the same (Peterson, 1983).

What does this have to do with social support? Well-functioning couples rely on effective communication and problem-solving skills to resolve conflicts (Jacobson & Margolin, 1979). Among these skills are behaviors that fall under the rubric of social support. Research by Gottman and colleagues illustrates this point. Gottman (1979) observed the behavior of distressed and nondistressed couples as they tried to resolve an issue on which they disagreed. Differences in behavior, including the use of supportive communications, distinguished distressed from nondistressed couples in all three stages of these problem-solving sessions.

In the early stage of the interactions, distressed and nondistressed couples differed quite markedly in the way they laid out issues for discussion. Among the distressed, a pattern of "cross-complaining" was frequently observed. One partner would voice a complaint and the other would respond with a complaint of his or her own. This pattern of mutual complaining went on and on, gathering emotional intensity as both partners became more and more angry and frustrated. By contrast, the nondistressed couples engaged in "validation sequences." One partner would voice a complaint and the other would validate the legitimacy of the expressed concern: "I can see why you were worried when I was out so late and didn't call." Then the second partner would express a concern of his or her own and would receive the same kind of validation: "I know you think I'm a worry wart—I do always think that the worst is going to happen." These validation sequences were much shorter than the cross-complaining exchanges of the distressed couples and they did not escalate nearly as much in emotional intensity.

The validation statements used by nondistressed couples appear to play a role in avoiding emotional escalation during conflict. These kinds of statements can easily be viewed as a type of social support. As described by Gottman (1979), they include expressions of sympathy, empathy, and understanding. They communicate a belief in the legitimacy of the other's feelings, thoughts, and actions. The ability (and willingness) to use such statements during disagreements appears to be a valuable asset in preventing the escalation of disagreements into highly destructive exchanges.

Gottman (1979) also observed differences in the verbal behavior of distressed versus nondistressed couples during the second phase of his problem-solving sessions. During the arguing phase, members of distressed couples repeatedly summarized their own feelings, views, and positions on issues: "I just can't take it when you blab about our private life. I've told you over and over again—don't talk about me to your sister!" By contrast, nondistressed spouses are more likely to summarize their partners' feelings, thoughts, and opinions: "You feel like I bad-mouth you to my sister all the time—and it makes you mad because you can't stand up for yourself and you don't think it's any of her business." Summarizing the other's communications is a way to demonstrate understanding and to assure the other that he or she has been heard. Such communications convey empathy and appear to facilitate smooth resolution of conflicts.

In the final phase of Gottman's (1979) problem-solving sessions, distressed couples engaged in a series of proposals and counterproposals that rarely converged on a mutually agreeable solution. Nondistressed couples also offered proposals and counterproposals but quickly agreed on solutions that took the desires of both partners into account. It appears that the ease with which they reached such compromises may in part be attributable to the more positive emotional tone that was maintained by the nondistressed couples. This more positive tone was maintained, in part, through the use of statements that validated and showed understanding of their partners' feelings and experiences, that is, social support. When people feel that their complaints have been given a fair hearing and that their feelings are understood, they are more willing to move from complaining to problem solving. If the discussion can be kept from deteriorating into inflammatory accusations, couples may be willing to compromise. Feeling less vulnerable, they may feel less need to protect themselves. Feeling less "wronged," they may feel less need to retaliate or punish the other with solutions that consider only their own well-being and desires.

Maintaining a positive or neutral emotional tone during disagreements between husbands and wives appears to be critically important. Gottman (1979) found that the greatest difference between distressed and nondistressed couples was the emotional tone of their discussions, especially nonverbal expressions of emotion (e.g., tone of voice, body language). The nondistressed couples could express their feelings in a neutral tone of voice—and could maintain this neutral tone even while disagreeing with their partners. Conflicts that arouse a high level of emotion—anger, fear, despair—can be highly destructive. Degree of physiological arousal during conflict predicted deterioration of the marital relationship over a 3-year follow-up period in a study by Levenson and Gottman (1985). Those couples who became intensely aroused during conflict showed significantly greater decreases in marital satisfaction at follow-up than those who did not become so aroused.

Fruzzetti and Jacobson (1990) argue that a high level of physiological arousal during conflict leads couples to withdraw from one another to avoid confrontation. As a result, problems are not resolved as they arise, leading to a stockpiling of hurts and resentments. When confrontations occur, their emotional intensity is very high. Thus, behavior strategies that promote open communication and a sense of being heard and understood by one's partner are extremely important—not only during times of crisis but during the normal daily transactions that make up life with a partner.

Promoting Trust, Intimacy, and Benign
Attributions for Negative Partner Behaviors

Social Support and Trust

Theorists have proposed that trust is built by repeated experiences in which the partner responds sensitively and consistently to the individual's needs, especially in times of duress (Holmes & Rempel, 1989). Once a schema of high trust is established—the confident expectation that the other will provide care in times of need—attributions for the individual's occasional negative behaviors become more benign. Rudeness or lack of consideration are attributed to external causes (e.g., forgetting a family outing because of pressures at work) or temporary internal causes (e.g., irritability due to lack of sleep). These benign attributions are less likely to lead to anger and conflict than attributions to stable characteristics of the individual (e.g., laziness or self-centeredness). Attributions for partner behaviors have been studied extensively by Fincham and his colleagues, whose research shows consistent differences between high- and low-conflict couples in the causal attributions they make for one another's behavior (Bradbury & Fincham, 1992; Fincham & Bradbury, 1990).

Social Support and Intimacy

If intensely negative emotional exchanges lead to relationship deterioration, it is also possible that intensely positive emotional exchanges contribute to relationship survival. Fruzzetti and Jacobson (1990) discuss the potentially powerful effects of intimate interactions on relationship maintenance. They define intimate interactions as those that "increase the understanding and vulnerability between partners and are accompanied by positive emotional arousal" (p. 127). They include interactions in which feelings about the relationship or the partner are expressed or in which emotions are expressed by one partner and accepted and understood by the other. Intimate interactions are relationship focused or self-revealing in content, not construed as an attack, and the importance of what is disclosed is appreciated by the listener, who responds in a positive, understanding, or self-revealing way. Such interactions often develop into a series of empathic and self-revealing exchanges. Intimate conversations result in increased closeness, understanding, agreement in the interpretation of events, and a sense of connectedness. Behaviors that fall under the rubric of social support appear to be critically important in facilitating intimate communication. Empathic statements that display concern and understanding are an integral part of intimate exchanges between partners.

Jacobson and Margolin (1979) discuss a "bank account" model of marriage, in which happy couples "build up" positive experiences with their spouses—intimate exchanges, pleasant times together, acts of kindness by the partner. With such experiences "in the bank," small offenses are less likely to cause major blowups because there is a large "balance" of goodwill and trust that is not depleted by a small "withdrawal." Intimate exchanges, by increasing the positive balance in the couple's relational "savings," may decrease marital partners' sensitivity to the other's occasional acts of unkindness or thoughtlessness because such transgressions occur within the context of a positive relationship.

The bank account metaphor is another way of describing the establishment of a positive relational schema. Moments of intense closeness and intimacy—fostered by supportive communications—contribute to a relational schema that includes highly rewarding experiences. Once again, it is likely that attributional processes play a role in the greater tolerance of individuals who enjoy a high level of intimacy in their marriage. Negative acts are attributed to benign causes that are temporary or externally controlled (Bradbury & Fincham, 1992; Fincham & Bradbury, 1990). Thus, conflicts are less likely to escalate out of proportion to the problem.

❧ Support Failures as a Source of Conflict: Disappointed Expectations for Support

A major source of distress in marriage is disappointed expectations. According to Sager (1976), all individuals enter marriage with an extensive set of expectations regarding how their partners would behave: For example, "He will love my mother." "He will always be strong and protect me." "She will always understand my moods."

According to Sager, these expectations are rarely articulated, and frequently, people are not aware that they hold them. When expectations are violated by the spouse, however, intense emotions are evoked.

One set of expectations concerns the partner's behavior during times of personal stress: "She will comfort me whenever I am sad or worried." Disappointed expectations for social support from the partner are a source of conflict in many relationships (Baxter, 1986). As noted in Chapter 1, expectations for both tangible and emotional assistance in hard times are a particularly important part of the implicit marital contract. The following example illustrates disappointed expectations for support.

After staying at work late to catch up on projects she couldn't finish because the day had been filled with demands and criticisms from her new supervisor, Sally was looking forward to pouring out her hurt, frustrations, and complaints to her husband, Jeff. She went over how she would describe her day to him while she was driving home and had a picture in her mind of how he would respond. This picture included fetching her a glass of wine, listening attentively, and sharing her indignation over the injustices of the day. When she walked into the living room, Jeff lowered his newspaper just long enough to snap, "Where have you been? It's almost 7 o'clock! How am I supposed to eat dinner and get ready in time for my bowling league at 7:30? You never told me what you wanted for dinner, and I've been waiting here for you to get home!"

Scenes such as this may not be unduly destructive if they occur infrequently. If individuals feel that their mate is consistently inattentive to their needs during times of adversity, however, considerable hurt and resentment can build up.

At least two different kinds of disappointments can occur regarding social support from the spouse. The first concerns the relative levels of resources that one receives and provides to the other in a relationship. There is evidence that perceived discrepancies between inputs and outputs in marital relationships predict lower marital satisfaction and higher rates of divorce (Austin & Walster, 1974; Davidson, Balswick, & Halverson, 1983; Walster, Berscheid, & Walster, 1973). According to equity theory, people are happiest when they view a relationship as equitable—each person gives and receives the same level of rewards. Both receiving less than one gives (underbenefit) and receiving more than one gives (overbenefit) lead to distress. In the case of underbenefit, distress is in the form of anger or resentment, whereas being overbenefited leads to feelings of guilt, shame, or obligation (Walster et al., 1973).

A second kind of disappointment has less to do with equity than with specific expectations for what a spouse should provide. Spouses may view certain behaviors as their partners' responsibility; these perceived responsibilities—emotional as well as instrumental— may differ for husband and wife. Thus, a husband may expect his wife to provide more nurturance than he provides to her, or a wife may expect her husband to provide an unemotional reaction to crises, even though she knows that her own reactions are intensely emotional. There is evidence that expectations for rewards play a significant role in reactions to the behavior of others, beyond considerations of equity (Austin & Walster, 1974).

❧ A Preliminary Investigation of Conflict and Support

In my laboratory, we have begun to examine the interplay between negative and supportive behaviors in the marital relationship. A study of married couples whose supportive and negative behaviors were observed and recorded is presented below. Because it illustrates the use of both self-report and behavioral indices of social support, it is described in some detail. The study posed the following three questions:

1. What are the relative contributions of supportive and negative behaviors to ratings of partner supportiveness?
2. What are the effects of inequitable levels of support provided by husbands and wives?
3. What are the effects of violations of expectations for support from husband or wife?

Participants were 100 residents of university married student housing (50 couples) who responded to a recruitment letter inviting them to participate in a study of communication and problem solving (Cutrona & Suhr, 1994). Participants ranged in age from 19 to 47 (mean = 27.0) and had been married from less than 1 to 11 years (mean = 3.0). Couples were asked to spend an evening in the laboratory completing a battery of questionnaires and participating in an interaction exercise, which was videotaped. Questionnaires included measures of perceived social support from the spouse, marital adjustment, personality, and depressive symptoms. In the interaction exercise, partners took turns disclosing a current source of personal distress in their life to their spouses. Each problem was discussed for 10 minutes. After each 10-minute interaction, the discloser completed a postinteraction questionnaire concerning the supportiveness of his or her spouse during the interaction and his or her overall satisfaction with the interaction.

Videotapes of these interactions were later coded by trained observers using the Social Support Behavior Code (SSBC) (Cutrona & Suhr, 1992; Cutrona, Suhr, et al., 1990; Suhr, 1990), which yields frequency counts of five different categories of supportive behaviors (emotional, esteem, information, tangible, and network support) and the frequency of negative behaviors (sarcasm, criticize, disagree, interrupt, complain, refuse request for help). In the current study, only the first four categories were analyzed due to reliability problems in the coding of network support. Mean interrater reliability (intraclass correlation) for the SSBC across the six major categories is .77, $p < .001$ (Cutrona & Suhr, 1992).

The interaction task was designed to elicit supportive behaviors. As expected, many more supportive behaviors than negative behaviors were observed. Women made an average of 17.00 supportive statements and 2.72 negative statements per 10-minute segment. For men, these figures were 18.00 and 2.30 respectively. Men and women did not differ significantly on the mean number of supportive behaviors displayed in any of the five categories or in the number of negative behaviors displayed. The frequency of supportive and negative behaviors displayed in an interaction did not correlate significantly ($r = .09$).

A note of caution should be introduced at this point. Because the interaction task was designed to elicit supportive behaviors, it is most informative about cooperative interactions between couples.

It is unlikely to elicit the most destructive behaviors in couples' repertoires and may be less informative about the effects of negative behaviors in tasks in which couples are placed in competitive or adversarial roles. This is an important point because most of the research on marital interaction that uses observational methods has placed couples in situations that maximize the likelihood of conflict and minimize the probability that they will exhibit highly supportive behaviors (Gottman, 1979; Margolin & Wampold, 1981; Rausch et al., 1974; Revenstorf et al., 1980). Thus, prior research may underestimate the potency of supportive behaviors, and the current study may underestimate the potency of negative behaviors.

Supportive and Negative Behaviors
Predicting Ratings of Support

Analyses were conducted to test the extent to which number of support behaviors and number of negative behaviors (both coded by observers) predicted participants' ratings of their spouses' supportiveness during the interaction. In addition, the personality of the individual in the role of discloser (extroversion and neuroticism scores) and his or her ratings of relationship quality (perceived spouse support and marital adjustment scores) were included in the regression equation. These variables were included to determine the extent to which factors outside the interaction contributed to people's evaluations of their partners' behavior in the listener role. For example, individuals who are high on neuroticism were expected to evaluate their partners' behavior more negatively than those with a low level of neuroticism (Watson & Clark, 1984). Similarly, individuals who were very dissatisfied with their marriage were expected to evaluate their partners' behavior in a negative manner. Four categories of predictors were tested: number of support behaviors received, number of negative behaviors received, personal characteristics, and relationship characteristics.

As shown in Table 4.1, number of supportive behaviors received from the spouse was a significant predictor of postinteraction supportiveness ratings. The more supportive behaviors displayed by the spouse, the higher the discloser rated his or her supportiveness during the interaction. Number of negative behaviors was not a

Table 4.1 Multiple Regression Predicting Postinteraction Ratings of Spouse Supportiveness

Predictors	R^2 Change	F Change	Standardized Beta[a]	r
Personal				
Extroversion			−.04	.07
Neuroticism			.15	.21
Depression			−.26*	−.36
	.13	4.87**		
Relationship				
Marital adjustment			.25	.49
Perceived spouse supportiveness			.12	.45
	.15	9.53**		
Spouse support behaviors				
Information			.08	.11
Tangible			.24*	.24
Emotional			.25*	.38
Esteem			.01	.28
	.13	5.05**		
Spouse negative behaviors	.01	2.13	−.12	−.20

R^2 Total = .42, $F(10, 89) = 6.57, p < .001$

NOTE: $N = 100$; *$p < .05$; **$p < .01$.
a. Final beta weights—that is, after all other variables have been entered into the equation.

significant predictor of postinteraction ratings of spouse support. These results did not differ by gender. Personal characteristics (especially depressive symptoms) and perceived quality of the marital relationship also contributed significantly to postinteraction ratings of partner supportiveness.

In the context of a cooperative interaction, negative behaviors occurred infrequently and had relatively little effect on individuals' evaluations of their partners' supportiveness. It appears that the context in which couples interact plays a major role in the salience of different classes of behaviors. In the context of a cooperative interaction, supportive behaviors are more important than negative behaviors as determinants of interaction supportiveness. Prior research suggests that negative behaviors are more salient determinants of satisfaction in the context of conflict interactions (Gottman, 1979). Care must be taken to avoid overgeneralizing context-specific results to relationship satisfaction more generally.

A second factor to be considered in evaluating the results of the current study is the relatively high level of marital satisfaction found among the participants. Research by Jacobson and colleagues suggests that maritally distressed and nondistressed couples attend to different kinds of spouse behaviors (Jacobson, Waldron, & Moore, 1980). Among distressed couples, the number of negative behaviors performed by the spouse each day is the strongest (negative) predictor of daily satisfaction with the marital relationship. Among nondistressed couples, however, the number of positive behaviors is the best predictor of daily satisfaction with the marriage. In our sample, which had few maritally distressed participants, supportive behaviors occurred most often and were the most salient. If a maritally distressed sample had been recruited, negative behaviors might have occurred more often and might have played a larger role in assessments of partner supportiveness.

Lack of Equity in
Support Behaviors Exchanged

The second question addressed was the extent to which equity in number of support behaviors given and received is a determinant of satisfaction with spousal support. Number of support behaviors was assessed using observer counts of supportive behaviors. A difference score was computed between the number of support behaviors received from the spouse when disclosing a personal problem and the number of support behaviors given to the spouse when he or she disclosed a personal problem. Positive scores reflected receiving more support than one gave (being overbenefited), and negative scores reflect receiving less support from the spouse than one gave (being underbenefited). According to equity theory, the highest level of satisfaction should occur when support received is equal to support given. Receiving more or less than one gives should lead to distress.

A multiple regression analysis was conducted to determine whether number of support behaviors received relative to number given was critical or whether absolute number of support behaviors received from the spouse was critical. In this analysis, only absolute number of support behaviors received attained significance. The difference between amount of support given and received did not predict supportiveness ratings when controlling for absolute number of support behaviors received. Furthermore, the prediction that perceived support would be highest when level of support received equaled level of support given was not confirmed. This nonlinear effect was not significant. Thus, the relative levels of support appears to be less influential than the absolute level of support received from the spouse in the context of disclosing a personal problem. The more supportive behaviors received, the higher the discloser rated his or her spouse's supportiveness, regardless of how this level of support compared to the level provided to the partner.

Violated Expectations
for Support From Partner

The next set of analyses examined the effect of receiving more or less support from the partner than expected. No specific measure of support expectations was administered. The general measure of perceived social support from spouse (Social Provisions Scale—Spouse Version) (Cutrona, 1989) that was administered before the interactions began was viewed as a reasonable approximation of support expectations. We reasoned that past experiences with the spouse would form the basis for responses to the perceived support scale—the same data that would shape expectations for support from the partner in the interactions. To express the expected support and received support scores using the same metric, we standardized each and then computed a difference score between what was received from the spouse (standardized number of support behaviors coded by observers) and what was expected from the spouse (standardized preinteraction Social Provisions Scale [SPS] score). Positive scores reflected receiving more than was expected and negative scores reflected receiving less than was expected.

Once again, we tested the prediction from equity theory that the highest level of satisfaction would occur when support received equaled the expected level (a nonlinear relationship). The results

Table 4.2   Multiple Regression Predicting Postinteraction Ratings of
Spouse Supportiveness From Difference Between Number
of Support Behaviors Received and Expected

Predictors	R^2 Change	F Change	Standardized Beta[a]	r
Number of support behaviors received	.06	5.89*	.47***	.24*
Difference between support received and expected	.08	8.71**	−.38**	
Difference^2	.05	5.89*	−.22*	−.22*

R^2 Total = .18, $F(3, 96) = 7.24, p < .001$

NOTE: $N = 100$; *$p < .05$; **$p < .01$; ***$p < .001$.
a. Final beta weights—that is, after all other variables have been entered into the equation.

were consistent with this prediction. As shown in Table 4.2, the
difference between expectation and support received was a significant predictor of interaction satisfaction. Those who received
more support than they expected were more satisfied with the
interaction. The square of the difference between expected and
received support was also a significant predictor of interaction satisfaction. This nonlinear term explained additional variance beyond
the absolute number of support behaviors provided.

To clarify the pattern of results, the data are graphed and
displayed in Figure 4.1. Support satisfaction was highest when
support received was slightly above the participant's expectation
level. Receiving either much more or somewhat less support than
expected was associated with lower support satisfaction. It is not
surprising that participants evaluated their partners' supportiveness negatively when they received less support than they expected. It is harder to explain why they evaluated their partners'
performance negatively when they received significantly more
than they expected. It may be that individuals believe that they
deserve a certain level of support and that receiving more makes
them feel guilty (Austin & Walster, 1974). People who are overbenefited in this way may feel pressure to increase the amount of
support they provide to their partners. Alternatively, receiving

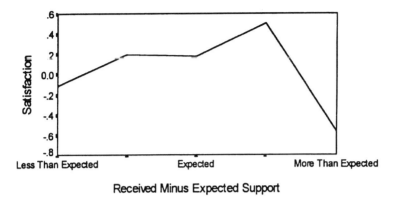

Figure 4.1. Predicting Interaction Satisfaction

more than expected may lead people to question their partners' motives—to make unstable, external attributions for their partners' behavior (Bradbury & Fincham, 1992; Fincham & Bradbury, 1990). They may attribute their partners' unexpectedly high level of supportiveness to a desire to show off in the presence of others or to embarrass them by behaving more supportively than they themselves did. Finally, it is possible that people simply do not like having their expectations violated!

❧ Conclusions

The utility of social support extends far beyond the narrow context of severe crisis situations. Supportive acts in the context of ordinary daily routines may contribute to a general sense of trust and goodwill, which decreases the probability that minor offenses by the partner will blow up into a major conflict. When disagreements arise between partners, supportive statements can prevent conflicts from escalating in emotional intensity. Supportive communications can also increase the frequency of rewarding interactions that increase feelings of closeness. These moments of intimacy may form the "glue" that keeps relationships intact through difficult times.

During times of severe stress, supportive acts may prevent emotional withdrawal. If partners can maintain emotional contact with one another when one or both are suffering, neither will feel alone in their efforts to confront and deal with problems. If adversity can be confronted as a team rather than individually, problems may be evaluated as less overwhelming.

A related dynamic is the role that a lack of support may play in creating relationship problems. People expect their partners to be supportive in times of stress. Disappointed expectations for support lead to dissatisfaction. Individuals feel uncomfortable when they receive more support than they expected, however. Support must be viewed as genuine and unselfishly motivated to be effective.

It is important to emphasize the interconnections between supportive and destructive behaviors—between intimacy and conflict. Neither positive nor negative behaviors can be adequately understood in isolation. Each sets the emotional stage for the other. A background of supportive acts can ease the sting of partner thoughtlessness. A background of coercive exchanges can undermine the best-intentioned supportive act. An intensely intimate self-disclosure that is met with validation and caring can strengthen a relationship so that it will later survive the strain of tragedy. Failure to provide the support that is needed during a crisis can lead to emotional withdrawal and the erosion of love.

Prior research has focused on the influence of social support on individual outcomes, such as adjustment and physical health. An exciting new direction is the study of social support's influence on relationships. It may be that the benefits derived by individuals from supportive interactions are due primarily to their effects on the quality, closeness, and trustworthiness of important relationships.

One context in which marital support is especially important is when one partner suffers from a serious or chronic illness. More research on marital social support has been conducted in this domain than in any other. Although the research comes from the health psychology literature, many of the issues that arise in the context of illness are generalizable to other chronic stressors. Special strains that tax the marital relationship are imposed by chronic stress. The role of social support in easing or aggravating such strains is addressed in the next chapter.

5

In Sickness and in Health
When One Partner
Has a Serious Illness

Beth remembers a scene between her parents during the final year of her mother's battle against cancer:

"My mother had lost almost 50 pounds—her stomach was constantly upset and irritated and her appetite was pretty much gone. One day she asked my father, who was doing all the housework and cooking by then, to make her some canned mushroom soup. She made a big point of telling him to stir it until the lumps dissolved. When he brought the hot soup to her 15 minutes later, she wept tears of rage and disappointment. 'It's lumpy! It's all full of big lumps! Didn't you stir it?' I had never heard either of them raise their voice to the other before. None of us knew what to do. My father took the offending soup back to the kitchen and threw it down the drain. He looked shaken and pale. For 2 days, he was withdrawn and tense. I hated the disease for what it had done to my gentle, loving parents."

Chronic illness changes the context in which social support is given and received in a number of important ways. The patient is placed in a position of dependence—options for "repaying" the well spouse for months or years of caregiving may be limited by virtue of physical disability, pain, and emotional exhaustion or turmoil. The well spouse, whose vision of the future never included caring for an invalid, may be overwhelmed with the demands of taking over the ill partner's household responsibilities, compensating for the ill partner's lost income, driving the partner to treatments, seeing the partner suffering, facing fears of the eventual loss of the partner, and coping with the emotional reactions of the partner to his or her condition. Whereas support may have flowed back and forth unnoticed between husband and wife before the onset of illness, an ever-growing imbalance may become intensely salient. Tensions can arise from such an imbalance, as well as from conflicts over the types of assistance that are helpful and those that threaten both the patient's dignity and her or his recovery.

Several key themes are highlighted in this chapter. First, the onset of serious illness is a crisis for both partners. Spouses are as much at risk for psychological distress as patients are (Coyne, Ellard, & Smith, 1990; Gillis, 1984; Kline & Warren, 1983; Thompson & Sobolew-Shubin, 1993). Second, both members of the couple must cope not only with their own distress but also with the emotions of their partners and the manner in which their partners try to cope with the situation. Third, for marriages to survive, couples must find a way to deal with the inequity that develops when one partner provides more support than the other. Fourth, open communication seems to be a critical component in maintaining a high-quality relationship in the context of serious medical illness. Finally, there is evidence that support from the spouse can backfire and interfere with the extent to which the patient regains strength and functional capabilities. A way of interacting must be found that neither reinforces the patient's helplessness nor ignores the sick partner's need for nurturance and understanding.

❧ The Importance of Spousal Support in the Context of Illness

For married persons, it is highly likely that the spouse will be the primary source of both physical care and emotional support in long-term illness (Ervin, 1973). Social support is a critical resource for persons who face serious illness. Longitudinal studies of cancer patients show that social support at the time of diagnosis predicts not only better emotional outcomes but longer survival times as well (Funch & Marshall, 1983; Vachon, 1979; Weisman & Worden, 1975). A number of studies have documented that women show better emotional adjustment after diagnosis of breast cancer if their husbands are highly supportive (Jamison, Wellisch, & Pasnau, 1978; Lichtman, Taylor, & Wood, 1987; Weisman, 1979). Among chronic pain patients, pain is less likely to lead to depression if the patient's spouse provides support (Kerns & Turk, 1984). For rheumatoid arthritis patients, support from the spouse is associated with better adjustment and the use of adaptive coping strategies (Manne & Zautra, 1989). It is important to discover the conditions that promote and interfere with the maintenance of a supportive marital relationship throughout the course of chronic illness.

❧ Interdependence of Emotional Reactions and Coping

Strong emotions are generated in both those who suffer from chronic illness and their spouses. Because of their interdependence, both members of the couple are affected not only by their own reactions to the illness but also by the emotional state of their partners (Kelley, 1979; Kelley & Thibaut, 1978). Among the well spouses of rheumatoid arthritis patients, both the patient's degree of disability and level of depression are stressors; both contribute significantly and independently to the well spouse's level of distress (Revenson & Majerovitz, 1991). This is consistent with the more general finding that life with a depressed partner is highly stressful and can lead to depressive symptoms in the nondepressed partner as well—a kind of emotional contagion (Coyne et al., 1987; Krantz & Moos, 1987).

Dealing With Anger

Depression is not the only emotion engendered by illness. Johnson (1990) describes anger as a common response to illness and an exacerbating agent in the illness process. A third of the well spouses

SOCIAL SUPPORT IN COUPLES

of arthritis patients name their partners' negative mood as one of the major stressors they face in daily life (Revenson & Majerovitz, 1991). As illustrated by the example at the beginning of this chapter, patient irritability can be extremely wearing on the well spouse.

Lane and Hobfoll (1992) conducted a longitudinal study of anger among couples in which one partner suffered from chronic obstructive pulmonary disease. Among patients, the severity of symptoms was a significant predictor of how angry the patients were. Those with more severe symptoms at the initial assessment reported higher levels of anger at the follow-up assessment 6 months later. The authors hypothesize that those with more severe symptoms had experienced more illness-related losses and accompanying declines in self-esteem, both of which have been linked in previous research to the emotion of anger (Feshbach, 1986).

Spouses of the pulmonary disease patients reported that the patients' irritability was a major source of stress. A significant link was found between anger in the patient and anger in the well spouse. Among couples in which the patients expressed anger openly, higher levels of anger were also reported by the well spouse. When patients reported feelings of anger but did not display these feelings openly, a delayed reaction in the spouse appeared to develop. Although the spouses did not show anger at the initial assessment, 6 months later their level of anger had risen significantly. Once again, a phenomenon of emotional contagion seems to occur.

Patient irritability is not the only trigger for resentment in the well spouse. The partner who is providing care may experience frustration over restrictions in his or her activities as a result of the patient's illness (Burish & Lyles, 1983). Recreational activities (fishing, golf, club meetings) may be abandoned by well spouses. Even if patients can care for themselves, they may complain of boredom or loneliness when left alone. Well partners may resent the patient's slow progress toward recovery, especially if they feel that the patient is not working hard enough to regain mobility and strength (Thompson, Bundek, & Sobolew-Shubin, 1990). A mixture of resentment and guilt are often reported by well spouses, who criticize themselves for not doing enough to help the patient (Bilodeau & Hackett, 1971), for focusing too much on their own needs, for resenting the patient's dependency or demandingness, or for their own irritability or firmness with the patient (Bilodeau & Hackett, 1971; Vess, Moreland, Schwebel, & Kraut, 1988).

Feelings of resentment may build up unexpressed in well spouses for long periods of time. They may be reluctant to express anger or resentment toward patients, who are already burdened with major life changes and losses, did not voluntarily become ill, and have no control over their illness (Thompson & Pitts, 1992). This simmering resentment may interfere significantly with the exchange of social support within the couple. The caregiver may fail to perceive the patient's need for support or may be unwilling to comply with requests for assistance (Cohen, 1978; Melamed & Brenner, 1990). Assistance that is provided may be given in a grudging manner or may be accompanied by criticism. As is described in a later section, there is evidence that the most resentful caregivers engage in the highest level of overprotective behaviors—performing tasks for the patient that he or she could do unassisted (Thompson & Sobolew-Shubin, 1993). At the same time, the well spouse's anger may interfere with her or his ability to obtain needed support. Unable to talk to the ill spouse about her or his feelings of anger and frustration, the well spouse may feel more and more emotionally isolated—cut off from her or his primary source of support (Thompson & Pitts, 1992).

It is clear that couples who are facing the stress of chronic illness must find constructive ways to manage their frustrations and resentments. Anger management is particularly critical because angry feelings are not only personally distressing but may also alienate potential support providers at a time when social support is needed most (Gates, 1980; Lane & Hobfoll, 1992). Both the patient and the well spouse stand to lose the support of the other if they let their frustrations and resentments fester without constructive airing and attempts to lessen the burden carried by each.

ἐ Interdependence of Coping

The success with which one partner copes with illness-related stressors is an important determinant of how well the other partner copes. Coyne and Smith (1991) term coping with chronic illness *a thoroughly dyadic affair.* In their study of couples in which the husband had suffered a myocardial infarction, the most adaptive coping strategy was not determined solely by the objective circumstances of the patient's condition but also by each partner's reaction to the patient's illness and the manner in which each partner tried to cope with the illness. The give-and-take between husband and wife as they tried to cope with the illness was a major determinant of the degree of disruption that was introduced into their lives by the patient's heart condition.

Coyne and Smith (1991) describe three central coping tasks faced by heart attack victims and their spouses: managing their own distress (emotion-focused coping), taking care of ongoing responsibilities and new tasks imposed by the illness (problem-focused coping), and dealing with the partner's presence and emotional needs (relationship-focused coping). A balance must be struck among these three coping requirements. At times, one's own emotional needs and those of the spouse can be mutually exclusive. For example, wives who protected their husbands from unpleasant news and problems in the day-to-day business of running the house and family suffer greater distress than wives who do not attempt to shield their husbands in this way. The husbands whose wives buffered them by withholding such news appeared to benefit, however. These husbands were more confident in their ability to cope with daily challenges than those whose wives did not protect them (Coyne & Smith, 1991, 1994). Women suffered from assuming sole responsibility for dealing with unpleasant or troublesome matters and from disguising their views to avoid conflict; but these same activities were associated with higher self-efficacy in their husbands!

Other examples of the interdependence of coping within couples can be found in the literature. Cronkite and Moos (1984) conducted a longitudinal study of couples who were facing a variety of adverse situations, including chronic illness. The personal characteristics and coping techniques of each member of the couple affected the coping and outcomes of the other. For example, when both husband and wife had high self-esteem, the wife's self-esteem was a more effective buffer against depression than when her husband was low on self-esteem. That is, the negative correlation between wife self-esteem and depression was stronger when her husband also had high self-esteem. A second significant interaction was found between husband self-esteem and wife coping style. Among men with high self-esteem, those whose wives tended to use avoidance coping were less protected from alcohol abuse by virtue of their own self-esteem than those whose wives did not use avoidance coping. It may be that the wife's tendencies to avoid rather than confront problems interfered with the husband's efforts to use effective problem-solving techniques or that her unwillingness to discuss problems with her husband placed an extra burden of emotional isolation on him, which led him to escape unpleasant emotions through alcohol.

Lichtman et al. (1987) examined the effects of how well each member of the couple coped with the wife's diagnosis of breast cancer. He found that the husband's rating of how well his wife coped was a significant predictor of his own marital satisfaction. An interviewer's rating of how well the husband coped with his wife's cancer predicted the couple's level of marital adjustment, even when controlling for retrospectively reported level of precancer marital satisfaction. Each partner's coping efforts affected the other's adjustment; the adjustment of each affected the rewards derived by both partners from the marital relationship.

❧ The Importance of Open Communication

A recurring theme in the literature on coping with chronic illness is the importance of open communication. Chronic illness can have deleterious effects on communication because the well spouse and other family and friends may believe that it is harmful for the patient to dwell on unpleasant topics (Dunkel-Schetter & Wortman, 1982). Relatives often believe that talking about the possibility of recurrence or death will hamper the patient's adjustment and might even lead to a recurrence or worsening of the disease (Lichtman et al., 1987). There is a tendency for the spouse and family of cancer patients to engage in "fair weather communication"—avoiding topics

that involve negative information or emotions (Vess et al., 1988)—
and to distract or discourage the patient from focusing on these
topics as well. This presents a dilemma for the patient who is seeking
social support. If she or he is not allowed to talk with loved ones
about current fears, resentments, or concerns, there is no opportunity to gain the comforts that derive from ventilating emotions
and feeling that another understands one's experience. In one study,
31% of breast cancer patients spontaneously expressed dismay over
their husbands' unwillingness to communicate about cancer-related
issues; 5% expressed the same complaint about other relatives and
friends (Lichtman et al., 1987). Evidence suggests that the open
expression of fears and sorrows may strengthen relationships. Studies
have found an association between open communication and marital satisfaction among couples in which one partner suffers from
chronic illness (Spiegel, Bloom, & Gottheil, 1983; Taylor, Lichtman,
& Wood, 1984). Among breast cancer patients, those who share their
concerns and report open and honest communication with their
husbands are better adjusted than those who keep their fears to
themselves (Lichtman et al., 1987). Rather than harming patients
psychologically, open discussion of death and other frightening or
unpleasant topics appears to facilitate adaptive coping.

Open discussion of threatening topics and negative emotions
seems to benefit the well spouse as well. Husbands of breast cancer
patients who are aware of their wives' anxiety and fear and who are
the most concerned about their wives' emotional reaction to the
disease are the most satisfied with their marriages (Lichtman et al.,
1987). Husbands who are aware of their wives' distress are probably
those who facilitate open expression. Because such disclosures by
the wife probably lead to similar disclosures of distress and fear by
the husband, both partners may benefit from the opportunity to
share their feelings. Such exchanges allow both partners to ventilate
their fears, express love and commitment, and increase in feelings
of closeness to their mate. As discussed in Chapter 4, the sense that
crises are faced as a team rather than alone may be an especially
important resource in times of severe stress. Although neither partner
can eliminate the threat that is causing their distress, facing the
future together may provide considerable comfort.

ᴥ A Difficult Challenge: Maintaining Equity

When one member of a couple develops a serious chronic illness, a dramatic shift is likely to occur in the balance of rewards and costs available to each individual in the relationship. As time goes on, the well spouse is likely to provide a proportionately larger share of rewards—taking on household chores, cooking, and child care responsibilities and assisting with self-care and medical regimens— as well as serving as the patient's primary link to the "outside world." With opportunities to gain reinforcements outside the home limited by pain, weakness, and other physical conditions, the patient may derive a very large percentage of opportunities for reinforcement through the well spouse. Thus, the marital relationship is likely to increase in rewards—and importance—for the patient. By contrast, the well spouse incurs a higher level of costs by virtue of her or his added responsibilities and may experience a drop in rewards due to the patient's physical limitations and emotional turmoil (Thompson & Pitts, 1992). As discussed in Chapter 4, inequitable relationships lead to distress for both the beneficiaries and the victims of the inequity (Walster et al., 1973). The person who is receiving a disproportionately large share of rewards may feel guilty, worry about becoming a burden, and feel anxious over potential abandonment by the partner whose share of the rewards is disproportionately small. The individual receiving disproportionately few rewards may experience anger or resentment—and become less committed to the relationship. Although both partners experience distress, according to equity theory, the intensity of distress should be greater for the partner who is receiving fewer rewards (Walster et al., 1973).

There is evidence that physical illness is more damaging to the marital satisfaction of the well spouse than to that of the patient. Among couples in which one member suffered from chronic pain, 25% of the patients and 65% of their spouses perceived a deterioration of their relationship as a result of the pain problem (Maruta, Osborne, Swanson, & Hallnig, 1981). Similarly, among stroke patients, patients had significantly more positive impressions of their partners than partners had of them; partners were significantly less likely than patients to report that the stroke had brought the couple closer together (Thompson & Pitts, 1992; Thompson et al., 1990). There is also evidence that after the onset of chronic illness, the relationship takes on greater importance for the patient and less importance for the well spouse. Among chronic pain patients, Kerns and Turk (1984) found a significant correlation between marital quality and depression. Patients with a high-quality marriage were less depressed than those with a poorer quality marriage. Among the spouses of these patients, the correlation between marital quality and depression was not significant; the quality of their marital relationship was not an important determinant of their well-being.

Although some couples break up as a result of serious illness in one partner, most do not. Although some disorders appear to be more damaging to relationships than others (e.g., chronic pain and disorders that impair cognitive ability), marriages are able to survive—and sometimes thrive—over long periods of time in the face of serious disability. How do couples handle illness-precipitated shifts in the relative benefits and costs of continued involvement with one another? It appears that a variety of strategies are employed by couples facing chronic illness to restore what Walster et al. (1973) term *psychological equity*. A number of these strategies are described by Thompson and Pitts (1992). For example, the couple may extend the time period over which equity is "computed"—they may focus on earlier benefits that were provided by the ill partner before the onset of illness (e.g., companionship, comfort, home care, child care, providing for the family's material needs). They may thus conclude that earlier rewards offset current costs. Couples may adjust the standards by which they judge the ill partner's contributions. They may take into account the limits of the ill partner's capabilities and, from that perspective, judge his or her contribution to be quite extraordinary: "Even though she's in pain, she always wants to know about my day and how it went. She acts like my problems are really important—even though they're pretty trivial compared to what she's facing." Couples may judge the ill partner's contribution by what he or she would be willing to do if roles were reversed and the other partner were ill: "I know he would do the same for me if I were sick." The ill partner may strive to provide increased benefits for the well spouse to compensate for benefits that he or she can no longer provide. An individual who can no longer work outside the home may take on new household chores that are not overly taxing. Efforts at providing emotional support and esteem support to the well spouse may be deliberately increased (Thompson & Pitts, 1992).

There is evidence that these strategies are successful for many couples. Lichtman et al. (1987) found that, in most cases, marital satisfaction remained relatively high in couples after the wife was diagnosed with breast cancer. In fact, husbands of breast cancer patients rated their marital satisfaction higher than the patients, even though their rewards were decreasing and their costs increasing —a finding that flies counter to social exchange theory predictions.

Insight into the ability of most couples to deal successfully with the apparent inequities that accompany chronic illness may be gained from several perspectives. First, it is important to conceptualize marriage as a relationship in which favors or benefits need not be repaid in kind—a communal rather than an exchange relationship (Clark & Mills, 1979). Neither member of the couple expects that a strict tally will be kept of services or favors provided. In a communal relationship, the partner who receives assistance is under no obligation to return a comparable benefit. To do so would threaten the belief that each partner should respond to the other's need—not out of obligation to repay a debt but out of love and concern. Thompson and Pitts (1992) interviewed couples on this issue. The well spouse of a stroke victim expressed his feelings as follows: "This is the way I feel, truly feel. After all, we've been married many years, we have lived together, we are companions, and we have a moral responsibility toward one another."

Another helpful perspective comes from interdependence theory. According to interdependence theory, people benefit not only from the goods and services they receive from relationships with others but also from the opportunity to display certain personal attributes or to see evidence of desirable personal attributes in the other (Kelley, 1979; Kelley & Thibaut, 1978). For the well spouse, providing care for the patient offers many opportunities to demonstrate positive attributes—supportiveness, commitment, kindness, love. According to Kelley (1979), these rewards are important to people above and beyond tangible benefits. For the patient, seeing such attributes in the spouse may ease the guilt and anxiety that accompany receiving a disproportionately large share of tangible rewards in the relationship. Another person can provide assistance for many reasons. Help can be seen as an expression of concern, a commendable sacrifice, the recipient's due, an attempt to manipulate, or a reflection of the receiver's dependence and incompetence (Gergen & Gergen, 1983; Jung, 1987). If the spouse's assistance is seen as motivated by positive intentions and love, worries over excessive dependency or negative evaluations by the well spouse can be greatly reduced (Thompson & Pitts, 1992). The rewards of displaying and perceiving positive traits and motives can compensate for inequalities of rewards in tangible benefits (Kelley, 1979). Of course, a relationship cannot continue in the complete absence of tangible benefits for either partner, but in many cases, the inequities imposed by illness can be managed through the psychological strategies described above.

A third perspective that may explain how couples deal with the inequities imposed by chronic illness concerns the tendency of spouses to idealize each other. In Lichtman et al.'s (1987) study of cancer patients and their spouses, both patients and spouses expressed the belief that their partners had suffered more than they had. This finding is consistent with research showing that marital partners tend to rate the other as "better" than the self and better than others in the same situation. Furthermore, spouses tend to rate their partners more positively on a variety of dimensions than their partners rate themselves (Berger & Kellner, 1964; Hall & Taylor, 1976; Taylor & Koivumaki, 1976). Lichtman et al. (1987) speculate that this idealization of the spouse is maintained by attributing the partner's positive behaviors (supportiveness, kindness, helpfulness) to stable characteristics of the person but attributing the partner's negative behaviors (impatience, irritability, forgetfulness) to characteristics of the situation. Once again, the importance of trust in the partner's goodwill and responsivity to one's needs is highlighted (see Chapter 1, this volume). If each person has a fundamentally positive relational schema, inequities imposed by the illness do not seem to damage the relationship seriously. Of course, if the couple was already experiencing problems in the relationship before the onset of illness—and does not have a positive relational schema characterized by high trust—cognitive strategies for accommodating to inequities in the rewards and costs of the relationship are less likely to be mobilized. Evidence suggests that the quality of the relationship prior to the onset of illness is a critical determinant of the extent to which chronic illness disrupts the marital relationship (Croog & Fitzgerald, 1978; Thompson & Pitts, 1992; Wellisch, Jamison, & Pasnau, 1978), although truly prospective studies have not been published (i.e., studies in which marital quality was assessed before the onset of illness).

❧ The Spouse Can Be a Source of Stress

The well spouse is not always a source of comfort. Marital partners of seriously ill patients can at times contribute to the patient's distress, exacerbate problems, or reduce the patient's motivation to recover or regain important functions (Coyne et al., 1990; Thompson & Pitts, 1992). One third of rheumatoid arthritis patients complained of unhelpful acts by family and friends—ranging from pessimistic comments about their prognosis to minimizing the severity of their illness (Affleck, Pfeiffer, Tennen, & Fifield, 1988). Spouses are sometimes quite critical of their ill partners. Women suffering from rheumatoid arthritis whose husbands were highly critical engaged in less adaptive coping behaviors and were less well-adjusted emotionally then those whose husbands rarely engaged in criticism (Manne & Zautra, 1989).

Wortman and her colleagues describe two different reasons for the hurtful behaviors that spouses and other close family members and friends direct toward persons suffering from serious illnesses. Illnesses such as cancer often generate feelings of fear and aversion, especially in those who have no previous experience with or exposure to serious illness. At the same time, as described above, many people believe that the most appropriate behavior toward a cancer patient is to maintain a cheerful optimistic facade. The conflict between these two reactions may lead to ambivalence and anxiety over interacting with the patient. Contradictory verbal and nonverbal behavior may be confusing or hurtful to the patient, who correctly detects a lack of genuiness (Wortman & Dunkel-Schetter, 1979). At worst, fear or discomfort may cause people to avoid the patient altogether.

A second source of "misfired" support may be differences in how the patient and the spouse think about the patient's disease (Silver & Wortman, 1980). In the case of breast cancer, for example, the husband may think of his wife as "cured" after successful treatment and expect her to recover her emotional equilibrium. The patient may have access to information that the spouse does not have—such as the continuation of lingering symptoms after treatment or information on rates of recurrence—that lead her to worry more about the future. The well spouse may compartmentalize the cancer, whereas the cancer pervades all areas of the patient's life. Finally, the well spouse may assume that the victim can voluntarily control her thoughts and emotions—"Just don't think about the possibility of recurrence! What good does it do to dwell on it?"—which are experienced as uncontrollable by the patient. The net effect may be impatience on the part of the well spouse, who views the illness as "behind us" after an apparently good response to treatment. The patient, however, may view the cancer as an ongoing concern and may be hurt and alienated by her spouse's insistence that she "stop worrying" and "get on with her life." The patient's preoccupation with her illness may be deeply unsettling to the spouse because it threatens his more benign assessment of the threat posed by her disease (Lichtman et al., 1987). The patient may not understand that the spouse's behavior reflects an effort to cope with his fears—thus, the emotional intensity of his insistence that "It's over! You're cured!" For an effective working relationship, both partners need to understand the other's way of thinking about the disease and the emotional ramifications of the partner's viewpoint. Without this understanding, a continuing spiral of well-intentioned but unappreciated attempts at support and mutually increasing feelings of resentment and emotional isolation can easily result.

❧ Overprotectiveness

Partners who overestimate the patient's physical and emotional recovery may push the patient to return to "business as usual" before he or she is ready. Some spouses make the opposite mistake of overprotecting the patient. Overprotection generally refers to underestimating the patient's capabilities, as manifested by unnecessary help, excessive praise for accomplishments, or attempts to restrict activities (Avorn & Langer, 1982). For chronically ill individuals, especially those who experience difficulty in self-care and functioning as autonomous adults, independence is an important issue. Overprotection by family members highlights patients' dependency and reduces their feelings of competence and control. It may even undermine their motivation to work toward their recovery (Avorn & Langer, 1982; Thompson & Pitts, 1992). Empirical support for the harmful effects of overprotection comes from several studies. Among 40 pairs of stroke patients and their spouses, perceived overprotection by the spouse was the strongest correlate of patient depression (Thompson, Sobolew-Shubin, Graham, & Janigian, 1989). The relation between overprotection and depression retains significance even when controlling for severity of stroke-related impairment. Similar results have been reported in other studies of stroke patients (Newman, 1984; Thompson & Sobolew-Shubin, 1993) and among cancer patients (Thompson, 1992).

The patient's self-image can also be damaged by spouse overprotectiveness. Spouse overprotectiveness predicts lower perceived control among stroke patients (Thompson & Sobolew-Shubin, 1993). Among heart attack victims, spouse overprotectiveness predicts lower self-efficacy (Coyne & Smith, 1994). Among the elderly, a curvilinear relation was found between the amount of social support received and locus of control scores (Krause, 1987). Up to a certain level, social support was positively associated with sense of control. Beyond that level, when support was excessive and probably reflected overprotection, the more support received, the lower the elderly person's sense of control.

Success in rehabilitation can be negatively affected by overprotection. Stroke patients who are overprotected by their family are less motivated to work in physical therapy (Newman, 1984). Even when controlling for initial level of impairment, Hyman (1971) found that chronically ill individuals with overprotective caregivers came to exhibit more disability than those who were not overprotected.

How much control the well spouse exerts over the behavior of the ill partner can become a hotly contested issue. Among couples in which one member had experienced an uncomplicated myocardial infarction, both patients and spouses expressed frustration with themselves and their partners over how they handled issues of control (Coyne et al., 1990). Arguments over the patient's failure to change diet and exercise habits and to avoid behaviors that might increase risk for another heart attack could become intense moral struggles. Well spouses often assert that the patient should engage in healthful behaviors and avoid risks out of obligation to them— even if the patient does not believe that the behaviors are beneficial. Well spouses feel both personally vulnerable—after all, they will be left alone if the patient dies—and an overwhelming responsibility to make sure that the patient does not endanger her or his health. This sense of responsibility at times seems to overwhelm considerations of their own well-being and the patient's need for autonomy and self-respect (Coyne et al., 1990). The patients in such relationships report that their spouses' attempts to control their behavior becomes their primary focus—overriding considerations of their own health and survival. At times, such patients become stubborn and even defiant, leading to major battles over what the patient should or should not do. Thus, intrusiveness of the well spouse into the daily behavior of the ill patient can take a toll on both partners. In fact, spouses showing the highest level of intrusiveness and overprotectiveness are the most likely to seek counseling or psychotherapy for themselves (Coyne et al., 1990).

What Causes Overprotectiveness?

Two studies have examined the antecedents of spousal overprotectiveness. Thompson and her colleagues tested several variables as predictors of the perception by stroke patients that they were overprotected by their spouses (Thompson & Sobolew-Shubin, 1993). These included negative caregiver attitudes toward the patient (feeling burdened by caregiving, believing that the patient did not try hard enough to regain lost functions), differences between caregiver and patient assessments of the patient's capabilities, and the frequency of helping behaviors undertaken by the well spouse for benign reasons (safety, convenience, patient well-being). Of all the variables tested, the only significant predictor of perceived overprotection was negative caregiver attitudes toward the patient. Such negative attitudes toward the patient were highest when the patient suffered from cognitive impairment or the caregiver had few sources of social support outside the marriage. Caregivers with few personal resources on which to draw and who were overwhelmed by the burdens of caregiving were the most likely to engage in intrusive, overprotective behavior.

Among couples in which the husband had suffered an uncomplicated myocardial infarction, the degree of burden experienced by the caregiver was once again a significant predictor of overprotectiveness (Coyne et al., 1990). In addition to caregiver burden, spouse overprotectiveness was also predicted by inadequate information from medical personnel before the patient's discharge from the hospital. Spouses who were not given adequate information on the patient's condition and activities that should be avoided versus those that posed no risk for another heart attack were more likely to behave in an overprotective manner. Low self-efficacy among the patients—discouragement and eroding morale—was a third predictor of spouse overprotectiveness.

Taken together, the two studies (Coyne et al., 1990; Thompson & Sobolew-Shubin, 1993) suggest that overprotection by the spouse is motivated by a number of different factors. Overprotection may be an indirect way of expressing resentment. Direct expression of frustrations to the patient may be viewed as unacceptable—after all, the patient did not deliberately become ill. In the absence of adequate social support, overburdened caregivers may have no outlet for expressing their frustrations and may express them in a passive-aggressive manner—by controlling the patient's daily activities. A desperate wish to keep the patient alive may motivate overprotective behaviors—even though such behaviors may actually lead to counterproductive behaviors by the patient and erode the relationship. A surprising finding from the Coyne et al. (1990) study is that the quality of the marriage prior to the onset of illness is unrelated to spousal overprotectiveness following the onset of cardiac disease. Thus, even in previously good relationships, spouses may become intrusive and restrictive. This transformation is more likely to occur when the spouse lacks specific information from medical personnel about how best to facilitate recovery. In the absence of such guidance, spouses appear to go overboard—imposing excessive restrictions and taking on too much responsibility for the patient's health. The tendency for spouses to take over such responsibility is also greater when the patient is discouraged and unsure of her or his own abilities. Well spouses may view their own intervention as critical in light of the patient's apparent lack of initiative—believing that if they do not protect the patient, no one will.

There is no easy way out of this dilemma for patients and their spouses. Given the powerful forces that propel caregivers to behave overprotectively, it is not surprising that this pattern is both widespread and difficult to change. Efforts to modify the well spouse's behavior must take into account the depth of emotions that underlly overprotectiveness and the needs of the well spouse for support and reassurance.

◈ Spousal Support as an Impediment to Recovery

Excessive interference and restriction by the well spouse can lead to misery for both patient and partner. There is evidence that, under some circumstances, even more subtle spouse behaviors can cause serious problems in the recovery process. When pain is a prominent feature of illness, a highly concerned and supportive spouse can actually prolong the duration of the patient's suffering and prevent the patient from attaining the highest possible level of rehabilitation.

From a role theory perspective, it has long been accepted that social roles—including the sick role—are socially determined (Parsons & Fox, 1958). A person is allowed to take on this role only with the agreement of significant others. Family members influence whether or not and how long an individual can adopt the sick role, for example, being excused from usual chores and social obligations (Parsons & Fox, 1958). Some of the ways in which families shape the behaviors of ill individuals can be understood from a behavioral perspective. Fordyce (1976, 1978) describes these processes as they apply to pain patients and their families. Behaviors that fall under the rubric of social support figure prominently in his formulation.

Attention, approval, sympathy, and other social rewards are seen as reinforcers that shape and maintain behavior. The spouse is in a particularly good position to provide or withhold these reinforcers —and thus can have a powerful effect on the ill partner's behavior. Fordyce (1976, 1978) describes the process through which social reinforcement from the spouse can actually encourage the development of chronic intractable pain. The transition from acute pain to a chronic pain condition is explained in terms of operant conditioning by the spouse. Pain behaviors are defined as acts that communicate that the patient is suffering, such as moaning, facial grimacing, and rubbing parts of the body. Initially, the expression of acute pain may be both adaptive and appropriate. Fordyce (1976, 1978) argues that when pain exists for a longer period of time, it may come under the control of external reinforcement contingencies, many of which are administered by the spouse. Expressions of pain may be reinforced directly, through attention and sympathy. If the patient lacks alternative means for obtaining reinforcement—if initiative and self-help attempts do not elicit social support from the spouse—the frequency of pain behaviors may accelerate rapidly. The patient's communication of discomfort may excuse him or her from undesirable activities, such as outside employment, household chores, or even sexual relations, thus increasing in frequency through the mechanism of negative reinforcement. Over time, the patient's pain behaviors can become maladaptive and lead to decreased activity, dependence on medication, and a general decrease in behaviors that lead to rehabilitation and resumption of normal functioning. Thus, social support (empathy, sympathy, tangible assistance) can backfire if it is provided in response to expressions of discomfort. In fact, the supportive spouse can become a discriminative stimulus for pain behavior in the patient (Block, Kremer, & Gaylor, 1980).

Evidence in support of Fordyce's (1976, 1978) model is quite convincing. In a hospital setting, when staff systematically withdrew attention to pain behaviors and reinforced well behaviors, activity level increased and use of pain medication decreased (Cairns & Pasino, 1977; Fordyce et al., 1973). How frequently the well spouse responded to patient pain was a significant predictor of severity of pain and the extent to which pain interfered with daily activities among chronic pain patients (Flor, Kerns, & Turk, 1984). Among rheumatoid arthritis patients, the more highly the spouse was rated by the patient on solicitousness, the more frequent the displays of pain behaviors by the patients (Williamson, Brenner, Robinson, & Melamed, 1989). Among pain patients with a highly solicitous spouse, patients displayed significantly more pain behaviors during an intake interview when in the presence of their spouses as compared to when the interview was conducted in the presence of a ward clerk (Block et al., 1980). Those with a nonsolicitous spouse displayed significantly fewer pain behaviors when the interview was conducted in the presence of their spouses than when it was conducted in the presence of a ward clerk.

When patient and spouse agree in their assessment of the severity of the patient's pain, the patient's treatment outcomes are poorer than when the spouse's assessment differs from that of the patient (Kerns & Turk, 1984; Swanson & Maruta, 1980). When the spouse believes the patient's expressions of pain, he or she probably finds it difficult not to respond with sympathy and offers of assistance. In the long run, however, such sensitivity and kindness are a disservice to the patient, who is not encouraged to make the efforts necessary to regain functional capabilities.

❧ Conclusions

Serious illness can introduce great strain into relationships—including problems in the give-and-take of social support. The illness is a crisis for both partners. Open communication appears to be a crucial component to successful coping. Partners should be encouraged to talk openly with each other about their problems, fears, and frustrations. Patients should be allowed to participate in the ups and downs of daily life as much as possible; spouses should not be afraid to seek emotional support for their own problems from their ill mate. Both may be overwhelmed periodically by the joint problems they are facing, but the evidence suggests that being overwhelmed together can lead to the mobilization of support for one another—and couples can gain strength from the knowledge that they are facing all problems as a team.

Fostering support "reinforcements" from outside the marital couple is also important. Well spouses with little social support of their own behave maladaptively, engaging in overprotective and intrusive behavior. Occasional respites from caregiving, a sympathetic ear outside the relationship, and assistance with the instrumental tasks of caregiving can all help ease the isolation and burden of the well spouse. For male caregivers, it may be more difficult to mobilize support outside the marriage because husbands traditionally rely almost exclusively on their wives for support. Thus, special efforts may be required to find sources of support that are acceptable to male caregivers.

Medical personnel have an important role to play in couples' adjustment to serious illness. Specific disease-related information and instructions regarding diet, exercise, and lifestyle changes should be provided to both the patient and the well spouse. In the absence of such specifics, it appears that spouses experience more personal distress—perhaps because of ambiguity regarding the level of vigilance required to maintain the patient's health, perhaps because the spouse feels alone in her or his efforts to care for the patient. The dangers of reinforcing pain behaviors should also be discussed openly by medical personnel. If the issue is framed in the context of fostering the patient's recovery, the caregiver may be less vulnerable to accusations of "not caring" or insensitivity for withholding sympathy or unnecessary assistance.

Different disorders bring somewhat different support-related problems. For example, chronic pain appears to foster more marital problems than other medical problems (Flor & Turk, 1984; Maruta et al., 1981). Support groups that focus on specific illnesses may be especially useful for couples in which one member is ill. Whenever possible, both patients and their spouses should be encouraged to participate in support and educational programs. The psychoeducational components of such support groups should offer information on relationship-related aspects of the illness as well as the more traditional medical education programs. If possible, skill-building components should be included in such programs—to help couples learn to communicate their fears, requests for assistance, and requests for independence—in a way that fosters closeness rather than separate suffering.

6

Social Support
Therapy With Couples

Bill and Kathy had lived in the same small college town for 12 years. They never thought they would move away until Bill received a job offer from a university in a larger city. The new position offered many opportunities for Bill, so they decided to move. Kathy, who had worked as the honors coordinator for the college where Bill had previously taught, was not able to find employment for many months after the move. The new university was more impersonal than the smaller school where she had worked before and showed little interest in helping Kathy find suitable employment. Kathy applied for many jobs but received no offers that interested her. Bill describes his failed efforts to be supportive to Kathy through this frustrating time:

"At first, we both believed that Kathy would find a job without any trouble. She had excellent recommendations and lots of experience working with students. But as the weeks and months dragged on and she wasn't offered anything but secretarial jobs, she started to get discouraged. I tried to help by suggesting people she should call or talk to. I even tried to get her to go back to school to retrain for some other kind of work. But it seemed like the harder I tried to be helpful, the madder she got. Finally, I started to get mad too. I thought she was being too picky about the jobs she was applying for. I

tried to tell her that, but she wouldn't listen. Every time I tried to help, she accused me of talking down to her. For the first time, we started fighting about money. I was just trying to be careful—we weren't bringing home as much when we were both working. After a while, it seemed like we were either fighting all the time or not speaking to each other. We had to get help, or I don't think we would have made it together through another year."

In the same way that people are not born with the knowledge of how to be good parents, we are not born knowing how to be supportive marital partners. A number of skills are involved in the process of requesting and providing social support. Like any other skills, they can be improved with "coaching" and practice.

Most behaviorally oriented marital therapies focus on decreasing the frequency with which marital partners engage in aversive behaviors, such as criticism, name-calling, and sarcasm. This is appropriate, given that distressed couples are more sensitive to negative than positive partner behaviors (Jacobson et al., 1980). Furthermore, when individuals harbor a high degree of resentment toward their partners, they may be unwilling to engage in supportive behaviors. Even if they do engage in such behaviors, there is a good chance that their partners will view them as insincere and suspect their motives. This suggests that if sessions devoted to building, practicing, and increasing the frequency of supportive communications were added to marital therapy, they would be most useful if introduced after basic conflict resolution strategies have been mastered and the frequency of aversive behaviors has decreased.

Alternatively, it might be best to teach the communication of social support as a preventive intervention. Supportive communications appear to function, in part, as a method of affect regulation. They generate a general climate of goodwill and trust and prevent negative interactions from escalating in emotional intensity. Thus, it is probably most useful to teach support skills early in relationships to prevent the deterioration of goodwill and the occurrence of damaging high-intensity conflicts. Once goodwill and trust have eroded, it is very difficult to restore them therapeutically. Marital therapists agree that one of the most difficult problems to reverse is the loss of love between partners (Geiss & O'Leary, 1981). Preventive interventions for dating couples or newlyweds that teach and emphasize the importance of supportive acts may allow some couples to maintain a generally positive emotional climate in their marriage and to avoid the erosion of love that is so difficult to reverse.

The use of supportive communications in a variety of contexts should be discussed, demonstrated, and practiced. Couples should learn to communicate their support expectations and needs to one another and to negotiate methods for "turn taking" when both are in need of support. The importance of maintaining emotional contact during times of stress and how to do so through supportive communications should be emphasized. Circumstances in which too much of certain kinds of support can undermine the self-efficacy of the other should be identified and discussed. The communication of social support is not a simple task and it should be taught explicitly, just as we teach methods of conflict resolution

Ideas for a marital intervention program that emphasizes social support are provided below. Topics are presented that could be included as part of a premarital preventive intervention or a marital enrichment program. Some sections may be appropriate as supplements to behaviorally oriented therapies for distressed couples. Alternatively, these topics could be presented to groups of couples who are facing a specific crisis in their lives to help them deal specifically with that crisis (e.g., diagnosis of serious illness in a family member; a natural disaster, such as a hurricane or flood; large-scale factory layoffs). Eight different themes are presented based on the theory and research presented in the first five chapters of this volume:

1. Social support is important.
2. Understand and respect differences.
3. Other people can provide support too.
4. Clear communication is important.
5. Use support skills during arguments.
6. Moments of intimacy—sharing private thoughts—are important.
7. Cope together with crisis or tragedy.
8. When one partner is ill, both partners need support.

In Table 6.1, a set of simply worded principles is listed under each general theme. Suggestions for ways to illustrate principles, including techniques and activities, are provided below.

❧ Social Support Is Important

In any intervention, it is important that the participants understand the underlying rationale. It may not be obvious to people why special training is needed in "being nice." As an introduction, it may be useful to discuss research findings on the link between social support and health—that large-scale epidemiological studies have shown that people who have high levels of support have fewer mental and physical health problems and live longer, even when taking into account other risk factors, such as smoking and cholesterol level (Berkman & Breslow, 1983; Schwarzer & Leppin, 1989). The importance of social support in building a strong marital relationship can also be highlighted. If support is consistently provided, trust between partners grows and deepens. Even when facing a minor problem, support from the spouse can make a difference. A sympathetic ear and a kind word build confidence that the partner really cares and can be relied on when serious problems arise. To illustrate the importance of support from the spouse, couples may be asked to think of an instance from their own life in which their partners were supportive in a time of stress or crisis. They may be asked to imagine how they would have felt and what would have happened to the relationship if their partners had not responded in a supportive manner.

The tendency for people to be more tolerant of one another's faults once they believe that their partners really care about their well-being should be emphasized. Most people have had the experience of a little annoyance building into a major conflict. If individuals have a history of consistent support from their partners, they are less likely to become enraged over minor instances of rudeness or lack of consideration. The bank account metaphor is useful in illustrating this principle. If a large balance of supportive behaviors is in the relationship bank, then a small withdrawal (e.g., an act of rudeness or inconsiderateness) does not deplete the

Table 6.1   Basic Concepts for a Preventive Intervention

Social Support Is Important
 1. We all need to know that someone cares enough about us to comfort and help us in times of stress.
 2. If our partner is not there for us in times of need, we feel especially hurt, angry, and disappointed.
 3. Do not wait for a big crisis to be supportive to your partner. Support following little everyday problems feels good and helps the relationship grow.
 4. If you are supportive of your partner when little things go wrong, your partner will trust that he or she can turn to you when serious problems arise.
 5. If you and your partner are consistently supportive of each other, you are more likely to forgive each other's small mistakes. Small problems in the relationship will not be blown out of proportion into big problems.

Understand and Respect Differences
 6. For some people, asking for help is easy. For others, it is almost impossible.
 7. Some people prefer to disclose negative events or problems to their partners right after they happen. Others prefer to wait until they think the situation over or make a start toward solving the problem.
 8. People cope with stress and tragedy in different ways. There is no right or wrong way to cope.
 9. It is important to understand how your partner copes with stress.
10. It is possible to learn from differences between how you and your partner cope with stress.
11. People prefer different kinds of social support. It is important to learn the kinds of support that your partner finds most comforting and helpful.

Other People Can Provide Support Too
12. It may not be possible to get all the kinds of support that you need from your partner. Find out what your partner can and cannot provide.
13. It is not necessary for your partner to meet all your needs for social support. Find out what kinds of support you can get from other people without damaging your marriage.

Clear Communication Is Important
14. Even if your partner doesn't know what is wrong, she or he will know that something is wrong.
15. If you don't tell your partner what is wrong, she or he may jump to the wrong conclusion.
16. If you don't tell your partner what is wrong, she or he can't help you deal with it.
17. People ask for support in different ways. Learn how your partner signals that she or he would like support from you.
18. Even people who have been married for a long time can't read each other's minds. Help your partner by communicating clearly what you want from her or him.

Use Support Skills During Arguments
19. Social support communication skills can be useful even during arguments. Listen, understand, and if possible, validate your partner's concerns.

Table 6.1   Continued

Moments of Intimacy—Sharing Private Thoughts—Are Important

20. Share positive feelings with your partner—about the relationship, about him or her, about the life you have built together.
21. Share your private thoughts with your partner—your hopes, your dreams, your disappointments.
22. Treat your partner's self-disclosures with care—listen, validate, empathize.

Cope Together With Crisis or Tragedy

23. In times of severe stress or tragedy, stay emotionally close to each other. Suffer together, cry together, shout together. Fight hard to stay close.
24. Fight the natural tendency to withdraw into your own private suffering. Force yourself to share your thoughts and feelings with your partner.
25. Plan a strategy for surviving the crisis together—take turns "falling apart"; make lists of people to whom you can turn for comfort, advice, and assistance; strive to make something meaningful out of the experience.

When One Partner Is Ill, Both Partners Need Support

26. If one of you becomes seriously ill, remember that your illness is also a crisis for your partner. Your health and survival affect him or her deeply.
27. If one of you becomes seriously ill, don't panic if you both experience a lot of anger. Illness isn't fair, and you deserve to feel angry.
    a. Be angry at the illness, not at each other.
    b. If you do feel angry at your partner, tell him or her what made you angry and why it upset you, as clearly and specifically as possible. Be constructive and try to work toward a solution of the problem.
    c. If your partner expresses anger toward you, try to listen and understand. Make your goals solving the problem and strengthening the relationship—not defending yourself or "winning."
28. If one of you develops a serious illness, talk openly about your fears for the future. Be afraid together, not apart.
29. If one of you is carrying a heavier load than the other because one of you is seriously ill, talk about how this inequity makes you feel. Find ways to "even the score" if the inequity is a problem for you.
30. If one of you has a serious illness, it may frighten or cause revulsion in your partner. Let your partner talk about it. Let your partner see that it's still you and that you still need him or her—but give your partner time to deal with his or her emotions.
31. If one of you has a serious illness, talk openly about the problem of the well spouse trying to be overprotective. Negotiate, compromise, set limits for each other. Be compassionate.
32. If one of you is in the process of rehabilitation after a serious illness or injury, openly discuss the best way to handle pain. Talk about the dangers of acting too sympathetic when the hard work of recovery causes pain. Provide encouragement. Praise achievements. Set aside a time to complain and give sympathy.

account. If nothing is in the bank to start with, any withdrawal may generate a crisis.

It should be emphasized that there are many different ways to provide support. In the example at the beginning of the chapter, Bill equated support with giving advice. As discussed in Chapter 4, advice is the type of support that is given most often and most often causes offense. Couples can be asked to make a list of different ways that they and their partners have been supportive of one another in the past. In a group setting, these lists can be shared with the group to illustrate the diversity of supportive acts. The five basic types of social support can be discussed as options that should be considered when the partner is in need (i.e., emotional, esteem, information, appraisal, and tangible support). The value of companionship—engaging in activities together to distract the partner from his or her problem temporarily—should also be discussed.

ᴥ Understand and Respect Differences

As discussed in Chapters 2 and 3, people differ markedly in how they react to adversity. These differences are sometimes associated with gender, but they may also spring from differences in culture, how problems were handled in families of origin, and a host of other temperamental and experiential factors. Regardless of their source, differences in the ways that members of a couple react to stress can cause frustration, hurt, and alienation at a time when partners need each other most.

How can couples deal with stylistic differences in their reactions to stress? The key elements of success are understanding and respect. Couples need to develop awareness and understanding of both their own approach to problems and that of their partners. They also need to realize that there is no one right way to deal with stress. Because the partner copes in a way that is different from one's own, that does not necessarily mean that the partner's way is wrong. (Some reactions to stress, such as excessive drug or alcohol intake, are maladaptive and should be dealt with directly through referral to an appropriate treatment program.)

To promote understanding of how individuals and their partners cope with stress, individuals may be asked to think of a recent stressful event in their lives and to write down a detailed account of how they reacted to it. These accounts should include the following:

1. Whether or not they disclosed the problem situation to anyone
2. Whether they waited or disclosed the problem immediately
3. Whether and how they asked for assistance or support
4. What they did to solve the problem
5. What they did to cope with their emotions

Partners should share their coping accounts with each other and identify similarities and differences.

Next, partners may be asked to think of a recent stress in their partners' life and describe how they perceive that their partners coped with the event, including the same information as in their personal coping accounts. Once again, these accounts should be shared with the partner. Individuals should have an opportunity to challenge the accuracy of their partners' view of how they reacted to the event. The purpose of this "accuracy check" is to identify possible misunderstandings and to allow individuals to describe what they were thinking and feeling when they reacted as they did. In the example below, Mary describes her husband's way of coping as "running away from problems into his work." Gerald's response is as follows:

> *"When I get involved in my work after something bad happens, it doesn't mean that I'm denying that there's a problem or refusing to deal with it. Thinking about something else for awhile and then coming back to the problem helps me get perspective. It seems like I even get ideas about how to work things out when I'm working on something unrelated to the problem."*

In a second example, Andrew says his wife Maria "falls apart" when problems arise. He says that it makes him feel like he has to "take over" for her at those times because she is too upset to think clearly. This is Maria's response:

"I know I'm a crier. I get really emotional at first when something goes wrong. It's like I have to face the worst that could happen. But that doesn't mean that I'm falling apart. After I get through that first stage of freaking out, I feel calmer and I get down to the business of taking whatever steps I can to improve the situation. You don't have to take over. You should just listen and be there. I'll be ready to deal with the nitty-gritty pretty soon. I'm not a baby."

Once couples have identified similarities and differences in their approaches to problems, several tasks remain. Couples should identify problems that arise as a result of their differences: "I feel abandoned when you go in to work whenever we get bad news from the doctor about Jill's medical condition." They should work together, with the assistance of the therapist, to figure out ways to deal with these problems: "I'll wait until you're feeling better to go to the office. Then, feel free to call me there if you need me, without feeling guilty. I'll let you know when I'll be home and when I get home, I'll listen to you for at least a half hour without contradicting you or telling you that you shouldn't feel the way you do." Compromising, taking turns listening and disclosing, giving each other time alone, communicating feelings, and reassuring the other of one's love and concern are all useful approaches dealing with differences in problem-solving style.

Couples should look for ways in which they may benefit from their partners' way of dealing with problems. For example, Randy found Diane's use of humor a relief from his tendency to analyze every detail of problems they confronted:

"I'd be going into these weird scenarios of 'What if this?' and 'What if that?' She'd say something really outrageous and bizarre, like 'I guess we could commit ritual suicide with the weed whacker' and I'd crack up."

Finally, couples should discuss what kinds of support they most like and appreciate from their partners. Husbands and wives may differ in their support preferences. We all have a tendency to give others what we ourselves would like to receive. We do not marry our identical twin, however, and it is important to have a good understanding of what our partner prefers to receive in times of stress: "I would hate it if you left me alone when I was upset. But you like time to think things out on your own, so I'll try to give you more space. Just make sure you let me know when you're ready to talk!"

Couples should be cautioned about the dangers of providing advice to one another. Research has shown that advice from the spouse is often unwelcome. Unless the stressed person specifically asks for advice or the partner has special expertise in the area causing problems, advice is the least preferred mode of support. By contrast, emotional support (expressions of love, caring, empathy, and concern) are welcome in virtually any circumstance. If individuals are uncertain what kind of support to offer, they should give emotional support.

◆ Other People Can Provide Support Too

Although the focus of this book is on the marital relationship as a source of social support, it is not realistic to rely on the spouse as one's only source of support. In some situations, the spouse may not be the best person to provide support. Some kinds of support may not be possible for the spouse to provide. Other demands on the spouse's attention and emotional energy may preclude the provision of support at a particular point in time. Multiple sources of support provide richness and variety in the kinds of support received. Thus, it is important to cultivate relationships outside the marriage that can provide support in times of need. One caution comes from Julien and Markman (1991), however, who found that seeking social support from sources outside the marriage at a time when the marriage was experiencing problems was associated with poor outcomes for the relationship. Problems in the relationship should be handled directly with the partner, with the assistance of a professional counselor, if needed.

To clarify potential sources of social support outside the marriage, individuals may be asked to list people to whom they could turn— for a sympathetic ear, for advice, and for tangible assistance—in each of a series of stressful circumstances. These circumstances might include problems at work, problems with extended family or children, financial problems, and serious illness of a family member. Individuals should be encouraged to think of family members,

friends, and coworkers, as well as professionals (physicians, coun-
selors, ministers). It may be useful to generate a list of people to
whom the couple could turn for support together in the event of
tragedy or extreme stress.

✄ Clear Communication Is Important

Standard behavioral techniques for building communication skills
can be applied to teaching and refining the skills involved in giving
and receiving social support (i.e., modeling the behavior, role-
playing, feedback, repetition, homework assignments to practice
skills in real-world settings). Skills should be broken into separate
components, including disclosure of distress to the partner, listening
nonjudgmentally to partner disclosures, providing each of the basic
types of social support to the partner (emotional, esteem, information, appraisal, and tangible assistance), requesting a specific type
of support, communicating that a different type of support is desired
than that provided by the partner: "I know you mean well, but I
really don't want advice right now. Can you just listen now, while I
figure out why I'm so upset over the situation?" and reinforcing
the partner for providing support (e.g., expressing appreciation or
thanks). Couples should discuss problems that are likely to arise in
the use of these skills and think of ways to prevent or handle such
problems: "It annoys me when you don't take me seriously when I
talk about my mother and how she's trying to run my life. If you'll
quit making jokes every time I bring up her name, I'll be clearer
about when I'm just irritated at her and when I'm really upset."
Skills that pose particular difficulty for a couple can be modeled first
by the therapist, who may play the part of one member of the couple
in a role play. Then the couple can try to role-play the skill on their
own, with coaching from the therapist if needed. To increase generali-
zation to real-world settings, behavioral homework assignments
can be given in which a particular skill is to be practiced at home
(e.g., describing problems that occurred at work to one's partner).
Problems that arise in these real-world practice sessions can be
discussed during the next session. Couples should be encouraged
to be flexible and tolerant of partner errors and to continue their
efforts at clear communication, even if initial results are discourag-

ing. They should show appreciation to their partners for support that is provided to reinforce these behaviors and increase the probability that they will occur in the future.

✦ Use Support Skills During Arguments

As discussed in Chapter 4, there is evidence that the use of supportive statements during arguments can help prevent small disagreements from blowing up into major battles. A number of excellent manuals are available for teaching couples how to "fight fair" (e.g., Bach, 1969). Such procedures may be supplemented with discussion of specific supportive communications that are useful in diffusing conflict. The most useful types of support in the context of conflict are probably empathic listening and validation—a type of esteem support. Validating the other's point of view does not necessarily imply that you agree with him or her but simply that you recognize the legitimacy of the partner's feelings and experience: "I can see why you were hurt by what I said. I really didn't mean it as a criticism, but I understand why you took it that way."

A technique used by many behavioral marital therapists to teach partners to listen to each other is to impose the "paraphrase before you respond" rule. Individuals must paraphrase or summarize what their partners have said before they may respond to the content of what was said. The individual who spoke may correct any inaccuracies in the partner's summary of what was said. This technique forces people to slow down and process what their partners are trying to communicate. This extra processing often yields increased empathy and willingness to validate the other's point of view. Hearing one's point of view accurately summarized is highly reinforcing and further increases willingness to hear and validate the other.

✦ Moments of Intimacy—Sharing Private Thoughts—Are Important

Early in romantic relationships, lovers frequently express their love for one another and confide their fondest hopes and dreams for the future. Such intimate moments of self-disclosure often decline as the relationship ages. Married couples should be encouraged to confide in one another—about their emotions, their wishes, their feelings for one another. Many marital enrichment programs provide structured opportunities for couples to engage in intimate communication with one another. As discussed in Chapter 4, such interactions are most rewarding when each person treats the self-disclosures of his or her partner with great care. Couples may be asked to disclose a positive feeling to their partners or a still-cherished ambition or a time that they felt especially close to their partners. Such confidences should be received with understanding, validation, and respect. Expressions of support in response to self-disclosure may increase feelings of closeness, love, and even romance.

✿ Cope Together With Crisis or Tragedy

Crisis or tragedy can strike any family. Sometimes, the damage that such a crisis inflicts on the marital relationship is as devastating as the original event. Research suggests that marriages are more likely to deteriorate if one or both partners retreats into private, solitary suffering—shutting out the partner and keeping grief locked up inside. Facing sorrow or disappointment alone is harder than facing it together with a partner. Couples who face crises as a team are more likely to emerge from their suffering with their marriage intact. Couples should be encouraged to share their grief with one another—to cry together, rage together, even feel hopeless together. Surviving the tragedy or crisis together should be a primary goal. To lose the marriage on top of the losses already suffered only compounds the tragedy.

Individuals should make a commitment to update each other regularly on their internal state: "I'm having a bad day. Yesterday, when the family was all here, I felt a little better, but today I really feel blue." Communication between marital partners is extremely important in times of crisis.

Couples should work out strategies to help each other deal with the crisis. For example, they may agree to help each other keep up their strength through eating healthy foods or exercising regularly. They may find ways to distract one another from their problems, such as seeing movies, going for walks, or reading aloud to one another. They may "take turns" being strong—allowing one or the other to "go to pieces" for a short period of time while the other carries on with daily responsibilities. They may work together to generate lists of people whom they believe can provide good advice on how to solve the practical problems that they face. They may generate lists of possible actions they can take to ease the source of their problem. They may pray together for guidance.

In the case of problems in which no solution is possible (e.g., the death of a loved one), they may seek to find meaning in their loss (e.g., establishing a memorial fund to be donated to a charity or to the hospital that cared for the patient in her or his final days). They may seek spiritual comfort together through their religious beliefs, perhaps seeking help from a trusted priest, minister, or rabbi. They may spend time with loved ones who can provide understanding and share their sense of loss.

Anxiety, grief, and depression may make it very difficult for individuals to reach out to their partners, seeking and offering support. If they can do so, however, they may be spared the searing pain of emotional isolation. The relationship may even grow in depth as a result of the experience.

❧ When One Partner Is Ill, Both Partners Need Support

It is easier to deal with a brief crisis than a long, extended strain, such as chronic illness. As described in Chapter 5, many difficulties arise in the give-and-take of social support when one member of the couple is seriously ill. Even though only one individual is sick, the illness is a threat to both partners, and both must make many adjustments in their lives. Thus, both members of the couple experience an increased need for social support, and both members are hampered in their efforts to provide support by the physical and emotional demands of the illness.

People often try to protect the ill partner from discussions of upsetting topics, especially when the illness is potentially life threatening. Patients express the need to talk about the possibility of disease recurrence and death, however. The well spouse may find such discussions doubly upsetting because they disrupt her or his own way of coping (i.e., denying that recurrence is possible). Nevertheless, if patients are not allowed to discuss their fears, they are prevented from receiving comfort and support. Experts such as Kubler-Ross (1969) advocate allowing patients to take the lead in discussions of death. If they want to talk about death, allow them to do so. If couples can cry together, they may also be able to find comfort, hope, and acceptance together.

If the spouse simply cannot face such a discussion, it may be best to ask the patient if there is someone else to whom she or he would like to talk about topics related to death (e.g., a minister or close friend). Similarly, well spouses may need to find someone in whom they can confide their own fears over the patient's death if the patient is unwilling to discuss the subject.

Clear communication can break down many barriers to smoothly flowing exchanges of support. Concerns over lack of equity in the relationship, fears that the partner's disease may be contagious, revulsion over disfigurement caused by disease or treatment—all become magnified if they cannot be discussed. Once articulated, they may lose their emotional intensity. Once again, there may be individuals outside the relationship who can serve as sounding boards for such self-disclosures, but problems within the relationship must be resolved within the couple. Professional help may be advantageous if partners find that they simply cannot communicate adequately with their partners in the context of serious illness.

Angry feelings sometimes take individuals by surprise when they are coping with their own or a partner's illness. Couples should be advised that such feelings are normal—there is nothing fair about serious illness and individuals have every right to feel angry about it. Sometimes, individuals mistakenly direct the anger they feel about the illness toward their partners. If possible, couples should strive to be angry together—at the illness.

Of course, in other situations, individuals are genuinely angry at their partners. People may be reluctant to confront their partners when the partner is ill, however, feeling that she or he already has enough to worry about. Although this reluctance to express anger is well intentioned, unexpressed anger may inhibit communication of all sorts, including the give-and-take of social support. Thus, it is probably best if people deal with angry feelings as they arise. Couples who are facing chronic or serious illness may benefit from training in how to express anger constructively. As mentioned previously, a number of treatment manuals and self-help books are available on how to handle conflict in a positive manner. Generally, couples are counseled to set aside specific times for conflict resolution, to limit discussion to the specific behavior or statement that made them angry, to avoid overgeneralizations such as, "You always . . ." or "You never . . ." to refrain from "zapping" one another with harsh criticisms, to practice active listening skills (e.g., the paraphrase-before-answering technique), to brainstorm together for solutions, and to seek solutions through negotiation and compromise (Jacobson & Margolin, 1979).

Techniques for dealing with conflict may be a valuable component for inclusion in psychoeducational support groups for couples in which one member suffers from a chronic illness, especially chronic pain. In the long run, it is probably not a kindness to conceal resentment toward the partner, even though she or he is coping with illness. The more skillfully such problems are dealt with, the less hurtful they will be and the sooner supportive behaviors can resume.

Couples must find ways to avoid "support" that damages rather than helps the patient cope or recover. Overprotectiveness on the part of the well spouse should be a major topic of discussion in support groups for couples in which one member faces a serious illness. Patients should be asked to describe specific behaviors by the partner that they perceive as overprotective. Partners may be asked to paraphrase what the patient said before responding to facilitate listening. Partners may then be given an opportunity to explain why they engage in the behavior, for example, their belief that the patient is insufficiently cautious or conscientious in protecting his or her own health. With the help of the therapist, couples should be helped to negotiate solutions to these conflicts. As in any other kind of conflict resolution, the emphasis should be on identification of specific behaviors that are problematic and specific solutions to problems. Negotiation and compromise should be encouraged: "I will cut back my jogging to 20 minutes a day. In return, I would like you to stop hiding the butter and let me eat what I want for breakfast."

A topic of discussion for support groups in which one member of the couple suffers from a chronic pain disorder is the problem of reinforcing pain behaviors. As described in Chapter 5, sympathy from the spouse can inadvertently lead to an increase in pain behaviors—including increased intake of pain medication, decreased activity level, and limited efforts toward rehabilitation. Patients and spouses should be made aware of the dangers of reinforcing or rewarding pain behaviors. Couples may try a variety of strategies to combat this problem. A specific time may be set aside daily for unlimited expressions of sympathy by the spouse—perhaps right before bed. The rest of the day, the spouse may be instructed to concentrate on reinforcing healthy behavior—praising the patient for efforts toward independence, for exercise, for trying to regain lost functions or mobility. Of course, it is important that both patient and spouse are well-informed about what the patient can realistically accomplish. Close communication with medical personnel is a necessity. Otherwise, both patient and spouse may become frustrated over continual failure to achieve unrealistic goals.

❧ Conclusions

Most social support interventions focus on building new relationships—"grafting" on new sources of social support. These interventions have met with limited success (Lakey & Lutz, in press). For those who are not truly socially isolated, a better approach may be to help people enrich existing relationships—to facilitate an increased flow of social support within marriages, families, and even friendship networks. A number of techniques for increasing the quality and frequency of social support behaviors within marital relationships have been suggested in this chapter (see also Lakey & Lutz, in press).

As a well-known marital therapist says, "People don't get married to manage conflict. They get married for companionship, intimacy, and support." To assist persons in obtaining and retaining these resources is clearly an important goal.

7

Future Research Directions

We have good evidence that a supportive relationship with an intimate partner is a significant asset. We do not know why, however, and we do not know how to help people who do not have adequate social support obtain it. In this volume, I have proposed that one of the primary mechanisms through which social support confers its benefits is through its positive effects on close relationships. I have argued that consistent responsivity to the other's needs within a close relationship fosters love, trust, tolerance, and commitment. All of these contribute to the stability of intimate relationships. The benefits of marriage for mental and physical health are outlined in Chapter 1. If social support increases the stability of marital relationships, its benefits are significant indeed. If social support further increases the quality of ongoing marriages, its benefits are even greater.

The goal of the research agenda that I propose is to gain insight into the role of social support in the development, quality, and

stability of intimate relationships. In this volume, I have proposed
a number of ideas along these lines, although little systematic data
have been gathered to test them. In this chapter, I offer suggestions
for research to clarify (a) how to conceptualize social support in the
context of other dimensions of close relationships, (b) the role of
social support in the development and maintenance of intimate
relationships, (c) the specific transactions that communicate support
effectively, and (d) the potential benefits of including social support
skills training in marital interventions. A variety of research methods
is needed to gain insight into the operation of social support within
marital relationships, including large-scale longitudinal studies
of couples, carefully controlled intervention studies, and micro-
analytic studies of support transactions in the laboratory. Each
method yields unique information that, when combined, may yield
important theoretical insights and offer direct clinical applications.

⊱ Conceptual Issues

We do not have a clear picture of how perceived social support
from the spouse fits into the larger constellation of characteristics or
dimensions of relationships. Can perceived support be empirically
differentiated from other dimensions? We do not know if measures
of perceived supportiveness capture a unique facet of relationships
or if supportiveness ratings can be entirely explained by some
combination of other characteristics (e.g., intimacy, emotional tone
of the relationship, frequency of conflict). Basic psychometric research is needed to clarify the place of social support in the overall
structure of close relationships. For example, is perceived social
support part of a higher-order construct of overall relationship
quality? Such a higher-order construct might be manifested in perceived supportiveness, compatibility, intimacy, ratings of communication quality, frequency and intensity of conflict, and the like. Does
perceived support from the spouse predict mental and physical
health outcomes or duration of the marital relationship beyond such
a higher-order marital quality construct?

If perceived social support can be differentiated from other facets of close relationships, the nature of its association with these other constructs must be clarified. At the present time, we do not know which dimensions of relationships are closely related to perceived support and which are orthogonal. In particular, we do not understand the relation between perceived supportiveness and negative aspects of the relationship. Are support and conflict different ends of the same continuum or orthogonal constructs? Do some couples report both high levels of support and high levels of conflict? Or are support and conflict mutually incompatible?

It is important that we understand the nature of the perceived spousal support construct. Otherwise, we may attribute personal and relationship outcomes to perceived social support that should more accurately be attributed to other related constructs (e.g., passion or infrequent conflict). Systematic research with large samples of married couples is needed to address such questions. Structural equation modeling techniques with latent variables should be used to obtain the clearest possible picture of relations among constructs.

❧ Social Support and the Developmental Course of Relationships

I have hypothesized that couples who establish a pattern of consistent responsiveness to their partners' needs (i.e., supportiveness) early in their relationship are more likely to develop a variety of positive qualities in their relationship over time, including mature or altruistic love, trust, intimacy, tolerance, and commitment. I discuss two methods for testing these predictions, correlational and experimental (i.e., controlled intervention) studies, below.

Support in Dating Relationships

Longitudinal studies are needed that track the development of relationships over time. Studies should examine the role of support in the progression of close relationships. It is not known whether supportive behaviors early in a dating relationship increase the probability that the relationship will progress from a casual to a more serious committed relationship. For example, what is the role of perceived partner supportiveness in the decision to marry? Both self-report and observational measures of social support should be used in these studies. The relation of behavioral (i.e., observed) support and perceived support to outcome variables may be different. For example, frequency of supportive behaviors may not predict relationship progression unless the partner is *perceived* as supportive.

Predictors of Social Support Early in Relationships

Early predictors of the development of support within relationships should be examined. For example, frequency and intimacy of self-disclosure may predict subsequent partner supportiveness (Derlega et al., 1993). Partners who readily disclose personal information to one another may create more opportunities for the provision of support than couples who do not readily self-disclose. Couples who experience stressful life events at the beginning of their relationship may also establish a pattern of mutual support early in their relationship. For example, if both partners are preparing to take an important exam (e.g., for entrance into medical or law school) or if one partner has a serious illness, supportive behavior may be woven into the fabric of the relationship from the start.

Individuals who received a high level of support from their parents while growing up may be more likely to provide support to their partners. For these individuals, supportive behaviors have been modeled extensively and support skills may have been acquired through observation. In addition, individuals who have observed the exchange of supportive behaviors in the home may view requesting and providing support as acceptable behavior to a greater extent than those who did not observe a free flow of support in their family of origin.

A range of personality variables undoubtedly influences people's ability and willingness to provide support to their relationship partner. For example, in my research, extroversion predicted the frequency of support behaviors provided by wives to their husbands (Cutrona & Suhr, 1994). Other fundamental personality characteristics should be examined in this regard as well (e.g., the remaining "big five" personality characteristics).

Consequences of Initial Level of Support

Studies are needed that trace the course over time of relationships that begin with high versus low levels of support. In these studies, multiple methods should be used to measure support, including self-report measures of perceived social support, daily diary studies of naturally occurring support behaviors, and observational studies of support transactions. These various indices of support should be tested as predictors of relationship characteristics over time. Outcome variables of particular interest include love, trust, closeness, interdependence, tolerance, commitment, marital satisfaction, and relationship stability. These analyses will be most informative if negative behaviors are also measured at the initial assessment (frequency and intensity of conflict, frequency of displeasing actions by the spouse, perceived discord, etc.). This will allow tests of whether support variables predict relationship outcomes above and beyond negative behaviors.

Of special interest are analyses that examine the extent to which initial support predicts the frequency and intensity of later conflict. As discussed in Chapter 4, evidence suggests that supportive communications during conflict reduce the intensity of negative emotion generated during conflict. It is not known whether people who are generally supportive of their spouses in nonconflict situations also use support skills in the context of conflict. It would be of interest to test whether level of perceived partner support predicts the use of validation statements during conflict and whether the use of such statements predicts lower-intensity conflict.

Changes in Marital Support

It is important to examine the degree to which changes in marital support are related to changes in other characteristics of the relationship. Research should investigate variables that are associated with increases or decreases in marital support over time. Three general categories of variables should be considered: normative life course events, nonnormative negative life events, and changes in the relationship.

A variety of normative life events may affect the level of support that marital partners provide to each other. Marriage, the birth of the first child, the oldest child entering school, the departure of the youngest child from the home, and retirement may all affect marital social support. Logically, it would seem that events involving increased responsibility (e.g., the birth of a child) would decrease frequency of marital support and that events involving decreased responsibility (e.g., last child leaving home, retirement) would increase the frequency of marital support. If either or both partners become depressed in response to a normative life change event, however, support from the depressed partner may decrease regardless of responsibility level.

Nonnormative life events (i.e., those that are not an expected occurrence in normal family development) may also affect the frequency and quality of support exchanged within marital couples. Acute events (e.g., injury suffered in a car accident) may lead to increased frequency of support from the spouse. There is evidence, however, that chronic stressors (e.g., unemployment) are followed by an initial increase and then a decrease in level of support received from the spouse (House, 1981). Research is needed on factors that predict continuing versus deteriorating support from the spouse following stressful life events.

Research on the interplay between support and other relationship characteristics is of special theoretical interest. Longitudinal studies are needed on the relation over time between social support and other aspects of relationships. For example, do changes in the frequency and quality of marital communication predict changes in perceived social support? What about changes in perceived quality of the sexual relationship? What is the effect on perceived support of changes in frequency of shared recreational activities?

Various attitudinal variables are presented in Chapter 1 as potential consequences of spousal support. These include love, trust, interdependence, a positive relational schema, tolerance, benign attributions for negative partner behaviors, and commitment. It would be of great interest to examine whether changes in social support are accompanied or followed by changes in these important relationship dimensions. Long-term longitudinal studies are needed to determine whether spousal support decreases the probability of relationship dissolution through the mediation of these variables.

Of particular interest is the relation between changes in support and changes in negative behaviors. Does increased conflict lead to decreased support? Does decreased support predict increased conflict? Does social support decrease the probability of marital dissolution through its influence on the frequency and intensity of negative behaviors?

Moderation by Gender and Personality

It is possible that social support is linked to other relationship dimensions somewhat differently for husbands and wives. In all studies, tests should be conducted to determine whether gender interacts significantly with support in the prediction of outcome variables. Other demographic characteristics may also moderate relations with social support (e.g., age, socioeconomic status). Tests should be conducted to determine the generality or specificity of effects to particular demographic groups.

It is also possible that social support operates differently for people with different personality characteristics. For example, a person who is high on neuroticism may not develop trust in response to supportive partner behaviors—or may develop trust more slowly than someone who is low on neuroticism. Research should systematically investigate interactions with selected personality characteristics. These characteristics should include the big five and other characteristics relevant to interpersonal relationships, such as degree of communal versus exchange orientation (Clark & Mills, 1979), level of dispositional trust (Holmes & Rempel, 1989), and security of adult attachment style (Hazan & Shaver, 1987).

❧ Understanding Social Support Transactions

A large and systematic literature documents differences between happily and unhappily married couples in the way they speak, act, and feel during arguments or disagreements with each other (e.g.,

Gottman, 1979). By inference, a fairly clear picture has evolved of what constitutes healthy versus unhealthy conflict behavior. Accordingly, behavioral intervention programs have been designed to increase healthy and decrease unhealthy conflict behaviors.

We do not know how happily and unhappily married couples differ in the way they speak, act, and feel when they are trying to help one another cope with stress. Thus, we have little empirical basis for concluding which kinds of support behaviors are adaptive and which are maladaptive. Studies are needed in which samples of maritally distressed and nondistressed couples are observed as they try to cope together with negative events. Comparisons between distressed and nondistressed couples should be made through all stages of the support process, including the disclosure of distress, requests for assistance, the provision of support by the provider, and expressions of appreciation (or rejection) by the support recipient. For example, individuals in distressed couples may use less effective support elicitation strategies, relying on indirect methods that are harder for their partners to read. Individuals in distressed couples may use a more negative tone of voice when requesting assistance, decreasing their partners' motivation to comply. Distressed and nondistressed couples may differ in the specific types of support they provide to each other—for example, members of distressed couples may give unwanted advice, whereas members of nondistressed couples may offer more emotional support. It is important to conduct careful comparative studies of nondistressed versus distressed couples as they try to be supportive to learn more about what enables the former to succeed and the latter to fail in their efforts to meet one another's needs.

Sequential analyses of support transactions may also yield useful information. Sequential analyses may help identify the utility of different support elicitation strategies. As a first step, a more detailed categorization system of the ways in which people try to elicit social support from their spouses must be developed. Once such a categorization system has been developed, it is possible to analyze support transactions between couples to determine what kinds of partner responses are most probable following each type of elicitation strategy. For example, the probability that an individual will receive emotional support from the partner following a direct request for sympathy can be compared with the probability that an individual will receive the same kind of support following an indirect support elicitation strategy, such as complaining. Once we know what kinds of support elicitation strategies lead to the most supportive response by the spouse, we will have an empirical basis for encouraging the use of such strategies in clinical intervention programs.

The effect of different kinds of support behaviors can also be investigated using sequential analyses. Exciting possibilities exist for assessing the emotional impact of specific support behaviors. These possibilities include analysis of the recipient's facial expressions (Izard, 1991), self-report of emotional reactions (Gottman & Levenson, 1985), and ongoing assessments of physiological reactions (Gottman & Levenson, 1986). For example, certain kinds of support behaviors may decrease autonomic arousal (most likely, emotional support) and other kinds of support behaviors may increase autonomic arousal (most likely, advice).

❧ Intervention Studies

A key question that remains largely unanswered is how to increase social support for those who do not receive enough support from the people around them. Chapter 6 provides suggestions for techniques to increase the quality and frequency of supportive behaviors within couples. Detailed treatment procedures should be developed and subjected to rigorous empirical tests, using random assignment to treatment conditions and multimodal outcome assessments (e.g., observation, daily diary data, and self-report questionnaires). In Chapter 6, three different contexts are suggested in which social support skills training would be most useful. The first context is as a preventive intervention for engaged couples (e.g., part of a marital preparation class or workshop). The second is as part of a psychoeducational support group for couples facing a particular common stressor (e.g., diagnosis of cancer in one member of the couple). The final context is as part of an intervention for distressed couples. Social skills training alone is not sufficient to meet the needs of any of the three groups listed above. Engaged couples, couples facing severe chronic stress, and maritally distressed couples all need a variety of different skills and information on a broad range of topics. For example, it is clearly necessary to provide communication and conflict management skills to engaged and maritally distressed couples. Well-designed empirical tests are needed to determine whether the addition of social support training to interventions can increase their effectiveness.

For example, one design might include the following conditions: communication training plus social support training, communication training only, social support training only, and no-treatment or contact control. In such studies, it is important to assess both final outcomes and mediating variables that may account for final outcomes. For example, final outcome variables would include marital satisfaction and marital stability (i.e., proportion of intact marriages in each condition at the time of long-term follow-up). Mediating variables would include social support and communication skill. In addition, theoretically predicted effects of increased social support and communication skill should be assessed as mediating variables, such as trust, interdependence, frequency and intensity of conflict, and commitment. If, for example, inclusion of a social support component in the treatment predicts a greater increase in perceived and observed supportiveness within couples, a greater increase in trust, and a greater decrease in intensity of conflict, then we can conclude that social support plays a causal role in the development of trust and control of negative affect during conflict. If the inclusion of a social support component in the treatment also predicts greater marital satisfaction at the time of follow-up (e.g., 5 years later), analyses can be conducted to determine if the social support treatment component increased marital satisfaction through its effects on trust and conflict intensity.

Intervention research of the type described above should be given high priority. It has the potential both to enrich and to improve the effectiveness of marital intervention programs. In addition, carefully designed intervention research provides the opportunity to test theoretically derived predictions about the mechanisms through which social support operates.

✿ Conclusions

I have proposed a number of new links between social support and other dimensions of the marital relationship. Far beyond the immediate comfort provided by a supportive word, I have proposed that supportive acts communicate important information about the partner and the relationship—that the partner can be trusted, that she or he is responsive to the individual's needs, and that the relationship will continue as a source of needed resources, refuge, and comfort. Once this information has been integrated into a stable relational schema, the stability of the relationship is greatly enhanced.

At this point, these ideas are largely theoretically based. The process of subjecting them to empirical test will be complex indeed. The information that results, however, will enrich our understanding of basic processes in close relationships, the health-promoting properties of social support, and how to help individuals reap the maximum possible benefits from their most important relationship.

References

Abbey, A., Abramis, D. J., & Caplan, R. D. (1985). Effects of different sources of social support and social conflict on emotional well-being. *Basic and Applied Social Psychology, 6,* 111-129.

Abramson, L. Y., Metalsky, G. I., & Alloy, L. B. (1989). Hopelessness depression: A theory-based subtype of depression. *Psychological Review, 96,* 358-372.

Abramson, L. Y., Seligman, M. E. P., & Teasdale, J. D. (1978). Learned helplessness in humans: Critique and reformulation. *Journal of Abnormal Psychology, 87,* 49-74.

Affleck, G., Pfeiffer, C., Tennen, H., & Fifield, J. (1988). Social support and psychosocial adjustment to rheumatoid arthritis: Quantitative and qualitative findings. *Arthritis Care and Research, 1,* 71-77.

Ainsworth, M. D. S., Blehar, M. C., Waters, E., & Wall, S. (1978). *Patterns of attachment: A psychological study of the strange situation.* Hillsdale, NJ: Lawrence Erlbaum.

Antonucci, T. C., & Akiyama, H. (1987). An examination of sex differences in social support among older men and women. *Sex Roles, 17,* 737-749.

Austin, W., & Walster, E. (1974). Reactions to confirmations and disconfirmations of expectancies of equity and inequity. *Journal of Personality and Social Psychology, 30,* 208-216.

Avorn, J., & Langer, E. (1982). Induced disability in nursing home patients: A controlled trial. *Journal of the American Geriatrics Society, 30,* 397-400.

Bach, G. R. (1969). *The intimate enemy: How to fight fair in love and marriage.* New York: William Morrow.

Baldwin, M. W. (1992). Relational schemas and the processing of social information. *Psychological Bulletin, 112,* 461-484.

Barbee, A. P. (1990a). Interactive coping: The cheering-up process in close relationships. In S. Duck & R. C. Silver (Eds.), *Personal relationships and social support* (pp. 46-65). London: Sage.

Barbee, A. P. (1990b). Separate processes in the relation of elation and depression to helping: Social versus personal concerns. *Journal of Experimental Social Psychology, 26,* 13-33.

Barbee, A. P. (1991, October). *The role of emotions and cognitions in the interactive coping process: Mood regulation in close relationships.* Paper presented at the annual meeting of the Society of Experimental Social Psychologists, Columbus, OH.

Barbee, A. P., Druen, P. B., Gulley, M. R., Yankeelov, P. A., & Cunningham, M. R. (1993). *Social support as a mechanism for the maintenance of close relationships.* Unpublished manuscript, University of Louisville, Louisville, KY.

Barker, C. (1984). The helping process in couples. *American Journal of Community Psychology, 12,* 321-336.

Barrera, M. (1981). Social support in the adjustment of pregnant adolescents: Assessment issues. In B. H. Gottlieb (Ed.), *Social networks and social support* (pp. 69-96). Beverly Hills, CA: Sage.

Barrera, M., Jr., & Ainley, S. L. (1983). The structure of social support: A conceptual and empirical analysis. *Journal of Community Psychology, 11,* 133-143.

Baxter, L. A. (1986). Gender differences in the heterosexual relationship rules embedded in break-up accounts. *Journal of Social and Personal Relationships, 3,* 289-306.

Beach, S. R. H., Fincham, F. D., Katz, J., & Bradbury, T. N. (in press). Social support in marriage: A cognitive perspective. In G. R. Pierce, B. R. Sarason, & I. G. Sarason (Eds.), *Handbook of social support and the family.* New York: Plenum.

Beach, S. R. H., Martin, J. K., Blum, T. C., & Roman, P. M. (1993). Effects of marital and co-worker relationships on negative affect: Testing the central role of marriage. *American Journal of Family Therapy, 21,* 313-323.

Belle, D. (1982). The stress of caring: Women as providers of social support. In L. Goldberger & S. Breznitz (Eds.), *Handbook of stress: Theoretical and clinical aspects* (pp. 496-505). New York: Free Press.

Belle, D. (1987). Gender differences in the social moderators of stress. In R. C. Barnett, L. Biener, & G. K. Baruch (Eds.), *Gender and stress* (pp. 257-277). New York: Free Press.

Berger, P., & Kellner, H. (1964). Marriage and the construction of reality. *Diogenes, 46,* 1-25.

Berkman, L. F., & Breslow, L. (1983). *Health and ways of living: Findings from the Alameda County Study.* New York: Oxford University Press.

Berkman, L. F., & Syme, L. (1979). Social networks, host resistance, and mortality: A nine-year follow-up study of Alameda County residents. *American Journal of Epidemiology, 109,* 186-204.

Berscheid, E. (1994). Interpersonal relationships. *Annual Review of Psychology, 45,* 79-129.

Berscheid, E., Snyder, M., & Omoto, A. M. (1989). Issues in studying close relationships. In C. Hendrick (Ed.), *Close relationships* (pp. 63-91). Newbury Park, CA: Sage.

Billings, A. G., & Moos, R. H. (1982). Social support and functioning among community and clinical groups: A panel model. *Journal of Behavioural Medicine, 5,* 295-311.

Bilodeau, C. B., & Hackett, T. P. (1971). Issues raised in a group setting by patients of myocardial infarction. *American Journal of Psychiatry, 128,* 105-110.

Birchler, G. R., Weiss, R. L., & Vincent, J. P. (1975). Multimethod analysis of social reinforcement exchange between maritally distressed and nondistressed spouse and stranger dyads. *Journal of Personality and Social Psychology, 31,* 349-360.

Bird, H. W., Schuham, A. I., Benson, L., & Gans, L. L. (1981). Stressful events and marital dysfunction. *Hospital and Community Psychiatry, 32,* 386-390.

Block, A. R., Kremer, E. F., & Gaylor, M. (1980). Behavioral treatment of chronic pain: The spouse as a discriminative cue for pain behavior. *Pain, 9,* 243-252.

Blood, R. D., & Wolfe, D. M. (1960). *Husbands and wives: The dynamics of married living.* Glencoe, IL: Free Press.

Bowlby, J. (1969). *Attachment and loss* (Vol. 1). New York: Basic Books.

Bradbury, T. N., & Fincham, F. D. (1992). Attributions and behaviors in marital interaction. *Journal of Personality and Social Psychology, 63,* 613-628.

Braiker, H. B., & Kelley, H. H. (1979). Conflict in the development of close relationships. In R. L. Burgess & T. L. Huston (Eds.), *Social exchange in developing relationships* (pp. 136-168). New York: Academic Press.

Brown, G. W., & Harris, T. O. (1978). *Social origins of depression: A study of psychiatric disorder in women.* New York: Free Press.

Burish, T. G., & Lyles, J. N. (1983). Coping with the adverse effects of cancer treatments. In T. G. Burish & L. A. Bradley (Eds.), *Coping with the chronic disease* (pp. 159-189). New York: Academic Press.

Burke, R. J., & Weir, T. (1977). Marital helping relationships: The moderators between stress and well-being. *Journal of Psychology, 95,* 121-130.

Cairns, D., & Pasino, J. A. (1977). Comparison of verbal reinforcement and feedback in the operant treatment of disability due to chronic low back pain. *Behavior Therapy, 8,* 621-630.

Campbell, A., Converse, P., & Rodgers, W. (1976). *The quality of American life: Perceptions, evaluations, and satisfactions.* New York: Russell Sage.

Caplan, G. (1974). *Support systems and community mental health: Lectures on conceptual development.* New York: Behavioral Publications.

Cassel, J. (1974). Psychosocial processes and "stress": Theoretical formulations. *International Journal of Health Services, 4,* 471-482.

Chesler, M. A., & Barbarin, O. A. (1984). Difficulties of providing help in a crisis: Relationships between parents of children with cancer and their friends. *Journal of Social Issues, 40,* 113-134.

Christensen, A. (1988). Dysfunctional interaction patterns in couples. In P. Noller & M. A. Fitzpatrick (Eds.), *Perspectives on marital interaction* (pp. 31-52). Clevedon, UK: Multilingual Matters.

Clark, M. S., & Mills, J. (1979). Interpersonal attraction in exchange and communal relationships. *Journal of Personality and Social Psychology, 37,* 12-24.

Cobb, S. (1976). Social support as a moderator of life stress. *Psychosomatic Medicine, 38,* 300-314.

Cobb, S. (1979). Social support and health through the life course. In M. W. Riley (Ed.), *Aging from birth to death: Interdisciplinary perspectives* (pp. 93-106). Washington, DC: American Association for the Advancement of Science.

Cohen, S. (1978). Environmental load and the allocation of attention. In A. Baum, J. E. Singer, & S. Valins (Eds.), *Advances in environmental psychology* (Vol. 1, pp. 1-29). Hillsdale, NJ: Lawrence Erlbaum.

Cohen, S. (1988). Psychosocial models of the role of social support in the etiology of physical disease. *Health Psychology, 7*(3), 269-297.

Cohen, S., & McKay, G. (1984). Social support, stress, and the buffering hypothesis: A theoretical analysis. In A. Baum, J. E. Singer, & S. E. Taylor (Eds.), *Handbook of psychology and health* (pp. 253-267). Hillsdale, NJ: Lawrence Erlbaum.

Cohen, S., & Wills, T. A. (1985). Stress, social support, and the buffering hypothesis. *Psychological Bulletin, 98,* 319-357.

Coyne, J., & Smith, D. (1991). Couples coping with a myocardial infarction: A contextual perspective on wives' distress. *Journal of Personality and Social Psychology, 61,* 404-412.

Coyne, J. C., & DeLongis, A. (1986). Going beyond social support: The role of social relationships in adaptation. *Journal of Consulting and Clinical Psychology, 54,* 454-460.

Coyne, J. C., & Downey, G. (1991). Social factors and psychopathology: Stress, social support, and coping processes. *Annual Review of Psychology, 42,* 401-425.

Coyne, J. C., Ellard, J. H., & Smith, D. A. F. (1990). Social support, inter-dependence, and the dilemmas of helping. In B. R. Sarason, I. G. Sarason, & G. R. Pierce (Eds.), *Social support: An interactional view* (pp. 129-149). New York: John Wiley.

Coyne, J. C., Kessler, R. C., Tal, M., Turnbull, J., Wortman, C. B., & Greden, J. F. (1987). Living with a depressed person. *Journal of Consulting and Clinical Psychology, 55,* 347-352.

Coyne, J. C., & Smith, D. A. F. (1994). Couples coping with myocardial infarction: Contextual perspective on patient self-efficacy. *Journal of Family Psychology, 8,* 1-13.

Coyne, J. C., Wortman, C. B., & Lehman, D. R. (1988). The other side of support: Emotional overinvolvement and miscarried helping. In B. H. Gottlieb (Ed.), *Marshalling social support: Formats, processes, and effects* (pp. 305-331). Newbury Park, CA: Sage.

Cronkite, R. C., & Moos, R. H. (1984). The role of predisposing and moderating factors in the stress-illness relationship. *Journal of Health and Social Behavior, 25,* 372-393.

Croog, S. H., & Fitzgerald, E. F. (1978). Subjective stress and serious illness of a spouse: Wives of heart patients. *Journal of Health and Social Behavior, 19,* 166-178.

Cutrona, C. E. (1986). Objective determinants of perceived social support. *Journal of Personality and Social Psychology, 50,* 349-355.

Cutrona, C. E. (1989). Ratings of social support by adolescents and adult informants: Degree of correspondence and prediction of depressive symptoms. *Journal of Personality and Social Psychology, 57,* 723-730.

Cutrona, C. E. (1990). Stress and social support: In search of optimal matching. *Journal of Social and Clinical Psychology, 9,* 3-14.

Cutrona, C. E. (1996). The interplay of negative and supportive behaviors in marriage. In G. Pierce, B. Sarason, & I. Sarason (Eds.), *Handbook of social support and the family.* New York: Plenum.

Cutrona, C. E., Cohen, B. B., & Igram, S. (1990). Contextual determinants of the perceived supportiveness of helping behaviors. *Journal of Social and Personal Relationships, 7,* 553-562.

Cutrona, C. E., & Russell, D. (1990). Type of social support and specific stress: Toward a theory of optimal matching. In I. G. Sarason, B. R. Sarason, & G. Pierce (Eds.), *Social support: An interactional view* (pp. 319-366). New York: John Wiley.

Cutrona, C. E., & Suhr, J. A. (1992). Controllability of stressful events and satisfaction with spouse support behaviors. *Communication Research, 19,* 154-176.

Cutrona, C. E., & Suhr, J. A. (1994). Social support communication in the context of marriage: An analysis of couples' supportive interactions. In B. B. Burleson, T. L. Albrecht, & I. G. Sarason (Eds.), *Communication of social support: Messages, relationships, and community* (pp. 113-135). Thousand Oaks, CA: Sage.

Cutrona, C. E., Suhr, J. A., & MacFarlane, R. (1990). Interpersonal transactions and the psychological sense of support. In S. Duck & R. Silver (Eds.), *Personal relationships and social support* (pp. 30-45). London: Sage.

Davidson, B., Balswick, J., & Halverson, C. (1983). Affective self-disclosure and marital adjustment: A test of equity theory. *Journal of Marriage and the Family, 45,* 93-113.

DePaulo, B. (1982). Social-psychological processes in informal help seeking. In T. A. Wills (Ed.), *Basic processes in helping relationships* (pp. 255-279). New York: Academic Press.

Derlega, V. J., Metts, S., Petronio, S., & Margulis, S. (1993). *Self-disclosure.* Newbury Park, CA: Sage.

Deutsch, M. (1969). Conflicts: Productive and destructive. *Journal of Social Issues, 25,* 7-41.

Duck, S. (1981). Toward a research map for the study of relationship breakdown. In S. Duck & R. Gilmour (Eds.), *Personal relationships: Personal relationships in disorder* (pp. 1-29). New York: Academic Press.

Duck, S. W., & Silver, R. C. (1990). *Personal relationships and social support.* London: Sage.

Dunkel-Schetter, C., & Bennett, T. L. (1990). Differentiating the cognitive and behavioral aspects of social support. In B. R. Sarason, I. G. Sarason, & G. R. Pierce (Eds.), *Social support: An interactional view* (pp. 267-296). New York: John Wiley.

Dunkel-Schetter, C., & Wortman, C. B. (1982). The interpersonal dynamics of cancer: Problems in social relationships and their impact on the patient. In H. S. Friedman & M. R. DiMatteo (Eds.), *Interpersonal issues in health care* (pp. 69-100). New York: Academic Press.

Eckenrode, J. (1983). The mobilization of social supports: Some individual constraints. *American Journal of Community Psychology, 11,* 509-528.

Eidelson, R. J. (1980). Interpersonal satisfaction and level of involvement: A curvilinear relationship. *Journal of Personality and Social Psychology, 39,* 460-470.

Ervin, C. V. (1973). Psychological adjustment to mastectomy. *Medical Aspects of Human Sexuality, 1,* 42-65.

Feshbach, S. (1986). Reconceptualization of anger: Some research perspectives. *Journal of Social and Clinical Psychology, 4,* 123-132.

Fincham, F. D., & Bradbury, T. N. (1990). Social support in marriage: The role of social cognition. *Journal of Social and Clinical Psychology, 9,* 31-42.

Fiore, J., Becker, J., & Coppel, D. B. (1983). Social network interactions: A buffer or a stress? *American Journal of Community Psychology, 11,* 423-439.

Flor, H., Kerns, R. D., & Turk, D. C. (1984). *The spouse and chronic pain: A behavioral analysis.* Unpublished manuscript.

Flor, H., & Turk, D. C. (1984). Etiological theories and treatments for chronic back pain: 1. Somatic factors and interventions. *Pain, 19,* 105-122.

Folkman, S., & Lazarus, R. S. (1980). An analysis of coping in a middle-aged community sample. *Journal of Health and Social Behavior, 21,* 219-239.

Fordyce, W. E. (1976). *Behavioral methods in chronic pain and illness.* St. Louis, MO: C. V. Mosby.

Fordyce, W. E. (1978). Learning processes in chronic pain. In R. A. Sternbach (Ed.), *The psychology of pain* (pp. 49-72). New York: Raven.

Fordyce, W. E., Fowler, R. S., Lehmann, J., DeLateur, B., Sand, P., & Treischmann, R. (1973). Operant conditioning in the treatment of chronic pain. *Archives of Physical Rehabilitation, 54,* 486-488.

Freedman, M. (1995). *The effects of marital quality, sense of control, and SES on psychological distress in the context of a natural disaster: A prospective study.* Unpublished master's thesis, Iowa State University, Ames.

Fruzzetti, A. E., & Jacobson, N. S. (1990). Toward a behavioral conceptualization of adult intimacy: Implications for marital therapy. In E. A. Blechman (Ed.), *Emotions and the family: For better or worse* (pp. 117-135). Hillsdale, NJ: Lawrence Erlbaum.

Funch, D. P., & Marshall, J. (1983). The role of stress, social support and age in survival of breast cancer. *Journal of Psychosomatic Research, 27,* 77-83.

Gates, C. C. (1980). Husbands of mastectomy patients. *Patient Counseling & Health Education, 2*(1), 38-41.

Geiss, S. K., & O'Leary, D. (1981). Therapist ratings of frequency and severity of marital problems: Implications for research. *Journal of Marital and Family Therapy, 7,* 515-520.

Gergen, M. M., & Gergen, K. J. (1983). Interpretive dimensions of international aid. In A. Nadler, J. D. Fisher, & B. M. DePaulo (Eds.), *New directions in helping* (pp. 329-348). New York: Academic Press.

Gillis, C. L. (1984). Reducing family stress during and after coronary bypass surgery. *Nursing Clinics of North America, 19,* 1103-1111.

Gotlib, I. H., & McCabe, S. B. (1990). Marriage and psychopathology. In F. D. Fincham & T. N. Bradbury (Eds.), *The psychology of marriage* (pp. 226-257). New York: Guilford.

Gottlieb, B. H. (1985). Social support and the study of personal relationships. *Journal of Social and Personal Relationships, 2,* 351-375.

Gottlieb, B. H., & Wagner, F. (1991). Stress and support processes in close relationships. In J. Eckenrode (Ed.), *The social context of coping* (pp. 165-188). New York: Plenum.

Gottman, J. M. (1979). *Marital interaction: Experimental investigations.* New York: Academic Press.

Gottman, J. M., & Levenson, R. W. (1985). A valid procedure for obtaining self-report of affect in marital interaction. *Journal of Consulting and Clinical Psychology, 53,* 151-160.

Gottman, J. M., & Levenson, R. W. (1986). Assessing the role of emotion in marriage. *Behavioral Assessment, 8,* 31-48.

Gottman, J. M., Markman, H., & Notarius, C. (1977). The topography of marital conflict: A sequential analysis of verbal and nonverbal behavior. *Journal of Marriage and the Family, 39,* 460-477.

Gove, W. R., Hughes, M., & Style, C. B. (1983). Does marriage have positive effects on the psychological well-being of the individual? *Journal of Health and Social Behavior, 24,* 122-131.

Hall, J., & Taylor, S. E. (1976). When love is blind. *Human Relations, 29,* 751-761.

Hazan, C., & Shaver, P. (1987). Romantic love conceptualized as an attachment process. *Journal of Personality and Social Psychology, 52,* 511-524.

Helmrath, T. A., & Steinitz, E. M. (1978). Death of an infant: Parental grieving and the failure of social support. *Journal of Family Practice, 6,* 785-790.

Hendrick, S. S., & Hendrick, C. (1992). *Romantic love.* Newbury Park, CA: Sage.

Hirsch, B. J. (1979). Psychological dimensions of social networks: A multimethod analysis. *American Journal of Community Psychology, 7,* 263-277.

Hobfoll, S. E. (1991). Gender differences in stress reactions: Women filling the gaps. *Psychology and Health, 5,* 95-109.

Holmes, J. G., & Rempel, J. K. (1989). Trust in close relationships. In C. Hendrick (Ed.), *Close relationships* (pp. 187-221). Newbury Park, CA: Sage.

House, J. S. (1981). *Work stress and social support.* Reading, MA: Addison-Wesley.

Husaini, B. A., Neff, J. A., Newbrough, J. R., & Moore, M. C. (1982). The stress-buffering role of social support and personal confidence among the rural married. *American Journal of Community Psychology, 10,* 409-426.

Huston-Hoburg, L., & Strange, C. (1986). Spouse support among male and female returning adult students. *Journal of College Student Personnel, 27,* 388-394.

Hyman, M. D. (1971). Social isolation and performance in rehabilitation. *Journal of Chronic Disease, 25,* 85-97.

Izard, C. E. (1991). *The psychology of emotions.* New York: Plenum.

Jacobson, N. S., & Margolin, G. (1979). Marital therapy: Strategies based on social learning and behavior exchange principles. New York: Brunner/Mazel.

Jacobson, N. S., Waldron, H., & Moore, D. (1980). Toward a behavioral profile of marital distress. *Journal of Consulting and Clinical Psychology, 48,* 696-703.

Jamison, K. R., Wellisch, D. K., & Pasnau, R. O. (1978). Psychosocial aspects of mastectomy: 1. The man's perspective. *American Journal of Psychiatry, 135,* 432-436.

Johnson, E. H. (1990). *The deadly emotions: The role of anger, hostility and aggression in health and emotional well-being.* New York: Praeger.

Julien, D., & Markman, H. J. (1991). Social support and social networks as determinants of individual and marital outcomes. *Journal of Social and Personal Relationships, 8,* 549-568.

Jung, J. (1987). Toward a social psychology of social support. *Basic and Applied Social Psychology, 8,* 57-83.

Kaplan, B. H., Cassel, J. C., & Gore, S. (1977). Social support and health. *Medical Care, 15,* 47-58.

Kaplan, D. M., Smith, A., Grobstein, R., & Fischman, S. E. (1973). Family mediation of stress. *Social Work, 18,* 60-69.

Kelley, H. H. (1973). The process of causal attribution. *American Psychologist, 26,* 107-128.

Kelley, H. H. (1979). *Personal relationships: Their structure and process.* Hillsdale, NJ: Lawrence Erlbaum.

Kelley, H. H. (1983). Love and commitment. In H. H. Kelley, E. McClintock, L. A. Peplau, & D. R. Peterson (Eds.), *Close relationships* (pp. 265-314). New York: Freeman.

Kelley, H. H., & Thibaut, J. W. (1978). *Interpersonal relationship: A theory of interdependence.* New York: John Wiley.

Kerns, R. D., & Turk, D. C. (1984). Depression and chronic pain: The mediating role of the spouse. *Journal of Marriage and the Family, 46,* 845-852.

Kessler, R. C., & McLeod, J. D. (1984). Sex differences in vulnerability to undesirable life events. *American Sociological Review, 49,* 620-631.

Kessler, R. C., & McLeod, J. D. (1985). Social support and mental health in community samples. In S. Cohen & S. L. Syme (Eds.), *Social support and health* (pp. 219-240). New York: Academic Press.

Kiecolt-Glaser, J. K., Dyer, C. S., & Shuttleworth, E. C. (1988). Upsetting social interactions and distress among Alzheimer's disease family caregivers: A replication and extension. *American Journal of Community Psychology, 16,* 825-837.

Kline, N. W., & Warren, B. A. (1983). The relationship between husband and wife perceptions of the prescribed health regimen and level of function in the marital couple post-myocardial infarction. *Family Practice Research Journal, 2,* 271-280.

Koch, A. (1985). "If only it could be me": The families of pediatric cancer patients. *Family Relations, 34,* 63-70.

Kohen, J. A. (1983). Old but not alone: Informal social supports among the elderly by marital status and sex. *The Gerontologist, 23,* 57-63.

Krantz, S. E., & Moos, R. H. (1987). Functional and life context among spouses of remitted and non-remitted depressed patients. *Journal of Consulting and Clinical Psychology, 55,* 353-360.

Krause, N. (1987). Understanding the stress process: Linking social support with locus of control beliefs. *Journal of Gerontology, 42,* 589-593.

Kubler-Ross, E. (1969). *On death and dying.* New York: Macmillan.

Kurdek, L. A. (1987). Sex role self schema and psychological adjustment in coupled homosexual and heterosexual men and women. *Sex Roles, 17,* 549-562.

Kurdek, L. A. (1989). Relationship quality in gay and lesbian cohabiting couples: A 1-year follow-up study. *Journal of Social and Personal Relationships, 6,* 39-59.

Lakey, B., & Lutz, C. (in press). Social support and preventive and therapeutic interventions. In G. R. Pierce, B. R. Sarason, & I. G. Sarason (Eds.), *The handbook of social support and the family*. New York: Plenum.

Lane, C., & Hobfoll, S. E. (1992). How loss affects anger and alienates potential supporters. *Journal of Consulting and Clinical Psychology, 60,* 935-942.

Lansky, S. B., Cairns, N. U., Hassanein, R., Wehr, J., & Lowman, J. T. (1978). Childhood cancer: Parental discord and divorce. *Pediatrics, 62,* 184-188.

Lazarus, R. S., & Folkman, S. (1984). Coping and adaptation. In W. D. Gentry (Ed.), *The handbook of behavioral medicine* (pp. 282-325). New York: Guilford.

Leatham, G., & Duck, S. (1990). Conversations with friends and the dynamics of social support. In S. Duck & R. C. Silver (Eds.), *Personal relationships and social support* (pp. 1-29). Newbury Park, CA: Sage.

Lefcourt, H. M. (1981). Locus of control and stressful life events. In B. S. Dohrenwend & B. P. Dohrenwend (Eds.), *Stressful life events and their contexts* (pp. 157-166). New Brunswick, NJ: Rutgers University Press.

Lehman, D. R., Ellard, J. H., & Wortman, C. B. (1986). Social support for the bereaved: Recipients' and providers' perspectives on what is helpful. *Journal of Consulting and Clinical Psychology, 54,* 438-446.

Lehman, D. R., Lang, E. L., Wortman, C. B., & Sorenson, S. B. (1989). Long-term effects of sudden bereavement: Marital and parent-child relationships and children's reactions. *Journal of Family Psychology, 2,* 344-367.

Leppin, A., & Schwarzer, R. (1990). Social support and physical health: An updated meta-analysis. In J. Weinman & S. Maes (Eds.), *Theoretical and applied aspects of health psychology* (pp. 185-202). London: Harwood.

Levav, I. (1982). Mortality and psychopathology following the death of an adult child: An epidemiological review. *Israeli Journal of Psychiatry and Related Sciences, 19,* 23-28.

Levenson, R. W., & Gottman, J. M. (1985). Physiological and affective predictors of change in relationship satisfaction. *Journal of Personality and Social Psychology, 49,* 85-94.

Levinger, G. (1983). Development and change. In H. H. Kelley, E. McClintock, L. A. Peplau, & D. R. Peterson (Eds.), *Close relationships* (pp. 315-359). New York: Freeman.

Libman, E., Takefman, J., & Brender, W. (1980). A comparison of sexually dysfunctional, maritally disturbed and well-adjusted couples. *Personality and Individual Differences, 1*(3), 219-227.

Lichtman, R. R., Taylor, S. E., & Wood, J. V. (1987). Social support and marital adjustment after breast cancer. *Journal of Psychosocial Oncology, 5,* 47-74.

Lieberman, M. A. (1982). The effects of social supports on response to stress. In L. Goldberger & S. Breznitz (Eds.), *Handbook of stress: Theoretical and clinical aspects* (pp. 764-784). New York: Academic Press.

Lin, N. (1986). Conceptualizing social support. In N. Lin, A. Dean, & W. Ensel (Eds.), *Social support, life events, and depression* (pp. 17-48). Orlando, FL: Academic Press.

Liotta, R. F., Jason, L. A., Robinson, W., & LaVigne, V. (1985). A behavioral approach for measuring social support. *Family Therapy, 12*(3), 285-295.

Lowenthal, M. F., & Haven, C. (1968). Interaction and adaptation: Intimacy as a critical variable. *American Sociological Review, 30,* 20-30.

Manne, S. L., & Zautra, A. J. (1989). Spouse criticism and support: Their association with coping and psychological adjustment among women with rheumatoid arthritis. *Journal of Personality and Social Psychology, 56,* 608-617.

Margolin, G., & Wampold, B. E. (1981). A sequential analysis of conflict and accord in distressed and nondistressed marital partners. *Journal of Consulting and Clinical Psychology, 49,* 554-567.

Maruta, T., Osborne, D., Swanson, D. W., & Hallnig, J. M. (1981). Chronic pain patients and spouses: Marital and sexual adjustments. *Mayo Clinic Proceedings, 56,* 307-310.

Maslow, A. H. (1968). *Toward a psychology of being* (2nd ed.). New York: Van Nostrand Reinhold.

McCubbin, H. I., & Patterson, J. M. (1983). Family adaptation to crises. In H. I. McCubbin, A. E. Cauble, & J. M. Patterson (Eds.), *Family stress, coping, and social support* (pp. 26-47). Springfield, IL: Charles C Thomas.

Melamed, B. G., & Brenner, G. F. (1990). Social support and chronic medical stress: An interaction-based approach. *Journal of Social and Clinical Psychology, 9,* 104-117.

Menaghan, E. (1982). Measuring coping effectiveness: A panel analysis of marital problems and coping efforts. *Journal of Health and Social Behavior, 23,* 220-234.

Newcomb, M. D. (1990). Social support by many other names: Towards a unified conceptualization. *Journal of Social and Personal Relationships, 7,* 479-494.

Newman, S. (1984). The social and emotional consequences of head injuries and stroke. *International Review of Applied Psychology, 33,* 427-455.

Nixon, J., & Pearn, J. (1977). Emotional sequelae of parents and siblings following the drowning or near-drowning of a child. *Australian and New Zealand Journal of Psychiatry, 11,* 265-268.

Oakley, G. P., & Patterson, R. B. (1966). The psychological management of leukemic children and their families. *North Carolina Medical Journal, 27,* 186-192.

O'Hara, M. (1986). Social support, life events, and depression during pregnancy and the puerperium. *Archives of General Psychiatry, 43,* 569-573.

O'Neil, J. M. (1981). Male sex role conflicts, sexism, and masculinity: Psychological implications for men, women, and the counseling psychologist. *The Counseling Psychologist, 9,* 61-80.

Parsons, T., & Fox, R. (1958). Illness, therapy, and the American family. *Journal of Social Issues, 8,* 31-44.

Pearlin, L. I., & McCall, M. E. (1990). Occupational stress and marital support: A description of microprocesses. In J. Eckenrode & S. Gore (Eds.), *Stress between work and family* (pp. 39-60). New York: Plenum.

Pearlin, L. I., & Schooler, C. (1978). The structure of coping. *Journal of Health and Social Behavior, 19,* 2-21.

Peterson, D. R. (1983). Conflict. In H. H. Kelley, E. Berscheid, A. Christensen, J. H. Harvey, T. L. Huston, G. Levinger, E. McClintock, L. A. Peplau, & D. R. Peterson (Eds.), *Close relationships* (pp. 360-396). San Francisco: Freeman.

Planalp, S. (1987). Interplay between relational knowledge and events. In R. Burnett, P. McGhee, & D. D. Clarke (Eds.), *Accounting for relationships: Explanations, representation and knowledge* (pp. 175-191). New York: Methuen.

Procidano, M. E., & Heller, K. (1983). Measures of perceived social support from friends and from family: Three validation studies. *American Journal of Community Psychology, 11,* 1-24.

Ptacek, J. T., Smith, R. E., & Zanas, J. (1992). Gender, appraisal, and coping: A longitudinal analysis. *Journal of Personality, 60,* 747-770.

Rabkin, J. G., & Streuning, E. L. (1976). Life events, stress, and illness. *Science, 194,* 1013-1020.

Rainwater, L. (1969). Sex in the culture of poverty. In C. Broderick & J. Bernard (Eds.), *Individual, sex, and society* (pp. 129-140). Baltimore: Johns Hopkins University Press.

Raush, H. L., Barry, W. A., Hertel, R. K., & Swain, M. A. (1974). *Communication, conflict, and marriage.* San Francisco: Jossey-Bass.

Repetti, R. L. (1989). Effects of daily workload on subsequent behavior during marital interaction: The roles of social withdrawal and spouse support. *Journal of Personality and Social Psychology, 57,* 651-659.

Revenson, T. A., & Majerovitz, S. D. (1991). The effects of chronic illness on the spouse. *Arthritis Care and Research, 4,* 63-72.

Revenstorf, D., Vogel, B., Wegener, K., Hahlweg, K., & Schindler, L. (1980). Escalation phenomenon in interaction sequences: An empirical comparison of distressed and nondistressed couples. *Behavioral Analysis and Modification, 4,* 97-115.

Rogers, C. (1942). *Counseling and psychotherapy: Newer concepts in practice.* Boston: Houghton Mifflin.

Rook, K. S. (1984a). Research on social support, loneliness, and social isolation: Toward an integration. *Review of Personality and Social Psychology, 5,* 239-264.

Rook, K. S. (1984b). The negative side of social interaction: Impact on psychological well-being. *Journal of Personality and Social Psychology, 46,* 1097-1108.

Rosario, M., Shinn, M., Morch, H., & Huckabee, C. B. (1988). Gender differences in coping and social supports: Testing socialization and role constraint theories. *Journal of Community Psychology, 16,* 55-69.

Rubin, Z. (1973a). *Liking and loving: An invitation to social psychology.* New York: Holt, Rinehart & Winston.

Rubin, Z. (1973b). Measurement of romantic love. *Journal of Personality and Social Psychology, 16,* 265-273.

Ruble, D. (1988). Changes in the marital relationship during the transition to first time motherhood: Effects of violated expectations concerning division of household labor. *Journal of Personality and Social Psychology, 55,* 78-87.

Russell, C. S. (1988). Marriages under stress: A research perspective. In E. W. Nunnally, C. S. Chilman, & F. M. Cox (Eds.), *Troubled relationships* (pp. 17-29). Newbury Park, CA: Sage.

Sager, C. (1976). *Marriage contracts and couple therapy: Hidden forces in intimate relationships.* New York: Brunner/Mazel.

Sarason, B., Sarason, I. G., Hacker, T. A., & Basham, R. B. (1985). Concomitants of social support: Social skills, physical attractiveness, and gender. *Journal of Personality and Social Psychology, 49,* 469-480.

Schenk, J., Pfrang, H., & Rausche, A. (1983). Personality traits versus the quality of the marital relationship as the determinant of marital sexuality. *Archives of Sexual Behavior, 12,* 31-42.

Schuster, T. L., Kessler, R. C., & Aseltine, R. H., Jr. (1990). Supportive interactions, negative interactions, and depressed mood. *American Journal of Community Psychology, 18,* 423-438.

Schwarzer, R., & Leppin, A. (1989). Social support and health: A meta-analysis. *Psychology and Health, 3,* 1-15.

Schwarzer, R., & Leppin, A. (1991). Social support and health: A theoretical and empirical overview. *Journal of Social and Personal Relationships, 8,* 99-127.

Shanfield, S. B., & Swain, B. J. (1984). Death of adult children in traffic accidents. *Journal of Nervous and Mental Disease, 172,* 533-538.

Silver, R. L., & Wortman, C. B. (1980). Coping with undesirable life events. In J. Garber & M. E. P. Seligman (Eds.), *Human helplessness: Theory and applications* (pp. 279-375). New York: Academic Press.

Simpson, J. A., Rholes, W. S., & Nelligan, J. S. (1992). Support seeking and support giving within couples in an anxiety-provoking situation: The role of attachment styles. *Journal of Personality and Social Psychology, 62,* 434-446.

Spiegel, D., Bloom, J. R., & Gottheil, E. (1983). Family environment as a predictor of adjustment to metastatic breast carcinoma. *Journal of Psychosocial Oncology, 1,* 33-44.

Steck, L., Levitan, D., McLane, D., & Kelley, H. H. (1982). Care, need, and conceptions of love. *Journal of Personality and Social Psychology, 43,* 387-411.

Stehbens, J. A., & Lascari, A. D. (1974). Psychological follow-up of families with childhood leukemia. *Journal of Clinical Psychology, 30,* 394-397.

Stokes, J. P., & Wilson, D. G. (1984). The inventory of socially supportive behaviors: Dimensionality, prediction, and gender differences. *American Journal of Community Psychology, 12,* 53-69.

Stone, A. A., & Neale, J. M. (1984). New measure of daily coping: Development and preliminary results. *Journal of Personality and Social Psychology, 46,* 219-239.

Suhr, J. (1990). *The development of the social support behavior code.* Unpublished master's thesis, University of Iowa, Iowa City.

Swanson, D. W., & Maruta, T. (1980). The family viewpoint of chronic pain. *Pain, 8,* 163-166.

Taylor, S. E., & Koivumaki, J. H. (1976). The perception of self and others: Acquaintanceship, affect, and actor-observer differences. *Journal of Personality and Social Psychology, 33,* 403-408.

Taylor, S. E., Lichtman, R. R., & Wood, J. V. (1984). Attributions, beliefs about control, and adjustment to breast cancer. *Journal of Personality and Social Psychology, 46,* 489-502.

Thoits, P. A. (1986). Social support as coping assistance. *Journal of Consulting and Clinical Psychology, 54,* 416-423.

Thoits, P. A. (1991). Gender differences in coping with emotional distress. In J. Eckenrode (Ed.), *The social context of coping* (pp. 107-138). New York: Plenum.

Thoits, P. A. (1992). Social support functions and network structures: A supplemental view. In H. O. F. Veiel & U. Baumann (Eds.), *The meaning and measurement of social support* (pp. 57-61). New York: Hemisphere.

Thompson, S. C. (1992). *Living with cancer.* Unpublished manuscript, Pomona College, Claremont, CA.

Thompson, S. C., Bundek, N. I., & Sobolew-Shubin, A. (1990). The caregivers of stroke patients: An investigation of factors associated with depression. *Journal of Applied Psychology, 20,* 115-129.

Thompson, S. C., & Pitts, J. S. (1992). In sickness and in health: Chronic illness, marriage, and spousal caregiving. In S. Spacapan & S. Oskamp (Eds.), *Helping and being helped* (pp. 115-151). Newbury Park, CA: Sage.

Thompson, S. C., & Sobolew-Shubin, A. (1993). Overprotective relationships: A nonsupportive side of social networks. *Basic and Applied Social Psychology, 14,* 363-383.

Thompson, S. C., Sobolew-Shubin, A., Graham, M. A., & Janigian, A. S. (1989). Psychosocial adjustment following a stroke. *Social Science and Medicine, 28,* 239-247.

Turner, R. J., Frankel, B. G., & Levin, D. M. (1983). Social support: Conceptualization, measurement, and implications for mental health. In J. R. Greenley (Ed.), *Research in community and mental health* (pp. 67-111). Greenwich, CT: JAI.

Vachon, M. L. S. (1979, August). *The importance of social support in the longitudinal adaptation to bereavement and breast cancer.* Paper presented at the annual meeting of the American Psychological Association, New York.

Vanfossen, B. E. (1981). Sex differences in the mental health effects of spouse support and equity. *Journal of Health and Social Behavior, 22,* 130-143.

Vanfossen, B. E. (1986). Sex differences in depression: The role of spouse support. In S. E. Hobfoll (Ed.), *Stress, social support, and women* (pp. 69-84). Washington, DC: Hemisphere.

Vaux, A. (1985). Variations in social support associated with gender, ethnicity, and age. *Journal of Social Issues, 41,* 89-110.

Vaux, A. (1988). *Social support: Theory, research, and intervention.* New York: Praeger.

Vaux, A., Burda, P., Jr., & Stewart, D. (1986). Orientation towards utilizing support resources. *Journal of Community Psychology, 14,* 159-170.

Veroff, J., Kulka, R., & Douvan, E. (1981). *Mental health in America: Patterns of help-seeking from 1957 to 1976.* New York: Basic Books.

Vess, J. D., Moreland, J. R., Schwebel, A. I., & Kraut, E. (1988). Psychosocial needs of cancer patients: Learning from patients and their spouses. *Journal of Psychosocial Oncology, 6,* 31-51.

Vinokur, A. D., & van Ryn, M. (1993). Social support and undermining in close relationships: Their independent effects on the mental health of unemployed persons. *Journal of Personality and Social Psychology, 65,* 350-359.

Vinokur, A. D., & Vinokur-Kaplan, D. (1990). In sickness and in health: Patterns of social support and undermining in older married couples. *Journal of Aging and Health, 2,* 215-241.

Walster, D. T., Berscheid, E., & Walster, G. W. (1973). New directions in equity research. *Journal of Personality and Social Psychology, 25,* 151-176.

Watson, D., & Clark, L. A. (1984). Negative affectivity: The disposition to experience aversive emotional states. *Psychological Bulletin, 96,* 465-490.

Weiner, B. (1980). A cognitive (attribution)-emotion-action model of motivated behavior: An analysis of judgments of help giving. *Journal of Personality and Social Psychology, 39,* 196-200.

Weisman, A. D. (1979). *Coping with cancer.* New York: McGraw-Hill.

Weisman, A. D., & Worden, J. W. (1975). Psychological analysis of cancer deaths. *Omega, 6,* 61-75.

Weiss, R. (1974). The provisions of social relations. In Z. Rubin (Ed.), *Doing unto others* (pp. 17-26). Englewood Cliffs, NJ: Prentice Hall.

Weiss, R. (1985). Men and the family. *Family Process, 24,* 49-58.

Wellisch, D. K., Jamison, K. R., & Pasnau, R. O. (1978). Psychosocial aspects of mastectomy: 2. The man's perspective. *American Journal of Psychiatry, 135,* 543-546.

Wethington, E., & Kessler, R. C. (1986). Perceived support, received support, and adjustment to stressful life events. *Journal of Health and Social Behavior, 27,* 78-89.

Wheaton, B. (1980). The sociogenesis of psychological disorder. An attributional theory. *Journal of Health and Social Behavior, 21,* 100-124.

Wheeler, L., Reis, H., & Nezlek, J. (1983). Loneliness, social interaction, and sex roles. *Journal of Personality and Social Psychology, 45,* 943-953.

Williamson, D. J., Brenner, G. F., Robinson, M., & Melamed, B. G. (1989, October). *Social influences on pain behavior in patients with rheumatoid arthritis.* Paper presented at the annual meeting of the American Pain Society, Phoenix, AZ.

Wong, M. M., & Czikszintmihalyi, M. (1991). Affiliation motivation and daily experience: Some issues on gender differences. *Journal of Personality and Social Psychology, 60,* 154-164.

Wortman, C. B., & Dunkel-Schetter, C. (1979). Interpersonal relationships and cancer: A theoretical analysis. *Journal of Social Issues, 35,* 120-155.

Wortman, C. B., & Lehman, D. R. (1985). Reactions to victims of life crises: Support attempts that fail. In I. G. Sarason & B. R. Sarason (Eds.), *Social support: Theory, research and applications* (pp. 463-489). The Hague, The Netherlands: Martinus Nijhoff.

Yankeelov, P. A., Barbee, A. P., Cunningham, M. R., & Druen, P. (1991, June). *Interactive coping in romantic relationships.* Paper presented at the International Conference on Personal Relationships, Normal, IL.

Index

About the Author

Carolyn E. Cutrona is a Professor in the Department of Psychology at Iowa State University. She also has an appointment at the Center for Family Research in Rural Mental Health at Iowa State. Prior to her present position, she was on the faculty at the University of Iowa for 12 years. A licensed clinical psychologist, she has taught graduate and undergraduate courses on depression, stress and coping, and marital and family therapy. She is currently a principal investigator on a large-scale collaborative longitudinal study of rural families that examines the role of community variables, network characteristics, social support, personal characteristics, and other factors in the prediction of mental health among both parents and children. She has studied social support processes in a number of stressed populations, including adolescent mothers, caregivers for Alzheimer's patients, spouses of cancer patients, and the elderly. She has published extensively in clinical psychology, social psychology, and interdisciplinary journals. She is a past Associate Editor of the

Personality Processes and Individual Differences Section of the *Journal of Personality and Social Psychology*. Her current interests include social support in marriage and families, observational methods for studying social support, and support processes in rural populations.